THE PERPETUAL WEALTH SYSTEM

I, Alan Stone, believe that John Jamieson is one of the best and most professional speakers I have seen or heard and I have participated in seminars in England and the U.S.A., where I live. A terrific performance!

—Alan Stone

Mr. Jamieson was recently facilitating a training class in real estate. His knowledge, experience, and communication skills really helped open my eyes and perception into new ideas, concepts and strategies into the real estate market. Mr. Jamieson's methods and strategies are tested proven and allotted economic gains for himself and his business. I highly commend his support, expertise, and facilitating techniques in the area of investing settings.

—Semi P. Saulo

I was at your seminar last weekend and I am writing to thank you for two days of great information. It was the most valuable seminar I have ever attended.

—Karen Harbrucker

You were one of the best (and most enjoyable) trainers that I've ever encountered (in any field)!

—Herb Brackman

THE PERPETUAL WEALTH SYSTEM

Your Path to Systematic and Guaranteed Riches

JOHN JAMIESON

NEW YORK

THE PERPETUAL WEALTH SYSTEM
Your Path to Systematic and Guaranteed Riches

Published in New York, New York, by Morgan James Publishing. Morgan James and The Entrepreneurial Publisher are trademarks of Morgan James, LLC. www.MorganJamesPublishing.com

The Morgan James Speakers Group can bring authors to your live event. For more information or to book an event visit The Morgan James Speakers Group at www.TheMorganJamesSpeakersGroup.com.

BitLit
FOR ALL THE BOOKS YOU OWN

FREE eBook edition for your
existing eReader with purchase

———————————————
PRINT NAME ABOVE

For more information,
instructions, restrictions, and
to register your copy, go to
www.bitlit.ca/readers/register
or use your QR Reader to scan
the barcode:

ISBN 978-1-61448-504-9 paperback
ISBN 978-1-61448-505-6 eBook
Library of Congress Control Number:
2013930339

Cover Design by:
Rachel Lopez
www.r2cdesign.com

Interior Design by:
Bonnie Bushman
bonnie@caboodlegraphics.com

In an effort to support local communities, raise awareness and funds, Morgan James Publishing donates a percentage of all book sales for the life of each book to Habitat for Humanity Peninsula and Greater Williamsburg.

Get involved today, visit
www.MorganJamesBuilds.com

Habitat for Humanity®
Peninsula and
Greater Williamsburg
Building Partner

Congratulations on ordering this book! I know it will be a life-changer for you and your family if you act upon the information you are about to learn. As a special thank you for your order I would like to send you an absolutely free gift of 3 very special CDs that will help you build and protect your wealth.

The first CD is called "Save a Fortune in Income Taxes." The biggest single expense most people have over a lifetime are income taxes and yet most people have no idea how they really work. We will show you how to give yourself an immediate pay raise by keeping more of what you make legally and ethically.

"How to make a fortune using the current housing crisis and foreclosure boom." I have been involved in tens of millions of dollars in foreclosure transactions and will share with you how to make your own fortune in the next 3 years. These are inside secrets known only to the most sophisticated investors.

"How to make a multiple six figure income by using Mega Marketing!" Most businesses fail because they just don't know how to get an abundance of clients or customers. No matter what business you are in, this CD will put more cash in your pocket right away.

These CDs will be rushed to you when we receive this filled out form. Please email or fax the entire form to info@perpetualfinancingsystem. com or fax to (586) 273-1507 and we will get the CDs rushed out to you right away. There is no cost or obligation. Thanks you again for your book order.

Yes John, Please rush me out my **FREE** information package including my 3 Free CD's

Name _____

Address_____

City _____

State_____ Zip Code _____

Phone number _____

Email address _____

John Jamieson
President of Perpetual Wealth Systems
www.perpetualfinancingsystem.com
www.johnjamieson.com
www.recashflowmachine.com

You are also invited to join our online community to hang out with John and his wealth strategists to remain current on wealth strategies. There are many hours of training on the site in the form of audio, video, and book trainings. New life changing material is available every month and you will have 24-hour access to all the information on the site once you join. You can have this huge resource in your life for far less than a cup of coffee every day. To get more details please visit www.perpetualwealthclub.com.

This book is dedicated to John and Dorothy Jamieson who were two of the best parents a person could hope to have. I am proud of both of you and wish you were here to see the book.

This is also dedicated to my wife Marybeth and sons John and Luke. I hope I make you as proud as you make me every day.

To all the people out there who have been told by the "powers that be" through your lifetime that you have to settle for less because they said so, nothing could be further from the truth. There are huge opportunities at your feet but you have to stop and look down. Find a vehicle and master it and go make your family's and your own life better than it is today.

TABLE OF CONTENTS

What others are saying about John and

THE PERPETUAL WEALTH SYSTEM

I first met John during a real estate training seminar back in November 2010. I was very impressed with John's knowledge of all aspects of real estate, but the concept of Perpetual Financing peaked my interest. I've been investing in stocks, all types of options, commodities, and currencies for more than fifteen years and I had never heard of the concept of Perpetual Financing.

My wife and I are currently using the funds in our whole life insurance policies to purchase four homes in Detroit this year at a discount from the peak market of 80% and renting them with a positive cash flow per month of $550.00. By pulling the funds from the policies, we continue to get the dividend on the total policy balance, plus the rental cash flow, plus the interest for using the funds goes directly back to our policies. Finally, all the earnings within the policy grow tax-free.

John and his team simplified and automated the entire transaction process. From setting up the whole life insurance policy, finding high quality properties in Detroit at great discounts, closing, taxes, insurance, renting to high quality tenants, and property management.

Finally, we plan to hold onto the properties for three to five years with the monthly positive cash flow and eventually sell the properties at an estimated 100% return, or more on our funds. John and his team will also handle the selling of the properties once the time is right.

A complete end-to-end solution.

Jay Hendricks
Washington State

"His Thinking is Forward and His Strategies Innovative"

The Perpetual Wealth System is the 21st century solution to everyone's financial well being. John's thinking is forward and his strategies innovative. After reading this book I quickly realized it's time for people in this country to realize there is a movement, a paradigm shift happening right before their eyes. People need to pay attention to how they are getting robbed by banks, Wall Street, and Uncle Sam. This new book lays out a financial life plan that will provide everyone liquidity and security with their finances for generations to come. Had I known about these simple yet powerful strategies years ago I would have many more assets for me and my family. I can't change my past but with this life changing information I can dramatically improve my financial future. Thanks for making the complicated topic of money so simple John.

Joe Militello

FOREWORD

The majority of my 20 plus year career has been spent in the financial industry, predominantly in the mortgage-banking arena. In that time I have happily paid to attend many great seminars to learn from the best of the best about marketing, selling, and positioning in the market place. I've had the privilege of seeing John Jamieson speak on several different topics since we first met in 2006 and every time I do, he hits one home run after another from the front of the room. No other expert I've discovered has been bold enough or dreamed big enough to tie together the incredible concepts of private banking with cash flow real estate which is where John shines the brightest. John has hit another one out of the park with this book, only this time it is a grand slam. Congratulations John on a job well done! I hope everyone will enjoy learning from you as much as I have.

Michael "Todd" Avery
Wealth Strategist

PREFACE

As I travel across North America and speak to thousands of people from all walks of life it becomes very apparent to me that people of all economic means struggle with the same basic money problems. I call those money problems "Wealth Drains" and there are 4 main ones in every persons and businesses life. If these wealth stealers are stopped or slowed down then every person and business will be able to acquire more wealth almost effortlessly. The Wealth Drains are:

1) Income Taxes
2) Money lost to downturns in the market
3) Interest and fees paid to banks and finance companies
4) Depreciation on large purchases such as cars

Ask yourself this simple question. How much more money would you have if you could cut your income taxes in half, never lose a dime in mutual funds ever again, paid no interest and fees to banks, and actually made money on items like your car or boat? The answer is you would have far more money than you do now. So let's stop those "Wealth Drains" and create wealth automatically and systematically month after month.

This book will challenge the age old teaching of maxing out your 401k and borrowing money from banks at low interest rates. We will show you that by using those age old teachings of the 401k and low interest rate loans you are making banks, Wall Street, and Uncle Sam rich while keeping you broke and don't even know why. This book will be the beginnings of a new and exciting path of wealth for you and your family. If you will act on the information you will not only create more wealth for you and your family today but will also help generations that you may not even know yet!

I don't care if you make $4,000,000 a year or $40,000 a year you are losing your own fortune to others needlessly and without even realizing the system is set up against you and your family. This book is the first step of turning all of that around. Once you read it reach out to my team so we can help you further.

Chapter One

WHY IS NOW THE PERFECT TIME FOR THIS BOOK?

As I write this book, we are in the middle of many uncertain times and events. The Stock Market is always a crap shoot, real estate values in most parts of the country are in the tank, unemployment is high, wages are stagnate, jobs have no security, gas prices are through the roof, savings rates are too low, and many other financial perils exist. Yet, with all of those problems, each one creates an equal or greater opportunity for the savvy businessperson and investor to make a fortune.

I am from metro Detroit and have lived here my whole life. This is arguably the hardest hit economy in the whole country. Most people here have a gloom and doom attitude about their financial future due to all of the reasons above and more that are unique to this locale. The biggest problem that Detroit has, along with most of the rest of the country, is not the hard economic times, but rather the lousy attitude that most Americans have adopted. We have been so conditioned that these economic times mean we can't make a great living and/or build wealth for our future. The truth is, there is a fortune at your feet in so many different areas, but you have to be looking for true opportunity. I will assume if you are reading this book or listening to this training program that you are in the very small minority that understands this is a golden opportunity to create wealth and fund your retirement years, so you can retire early and with your own personal fortune.

You see folks, it is not what happens to you that is important; it is what you think happened to you that is important. Most people in my town are so disgusted by the recent real estate collapse that they are afraid of real estate and don't see it as a wealth creator, but as a giant vacuum that sucks money out of your bank account. I must confess to you that I allowed myself to adopt this attitude for a short period of time. I had many investment properties and had made private loans in Metro Detroit and in Florida when both of those real estate markets collapsed. My personal net worth and income took a beating but more importantly than that, so did my attitude. Thankfully for me it was short lived and now I am back in wealth creation mode with both fists.

I can promise you that most of you are unaware (even residents of Detroit) that people from other parts of the world are flying into town to scoop up unbelievable bargains. How I know this is because I work with them every day in helping them to create a cash flow machine for themselves and their families. These savvy investors are parking money into high quality homes in nice, middle class areas. We will talk about this in detail in future chapters. I am bringing it up here just to illustrate how people can be right in front of an opportunity and not even see it, mostly because they do not want to see it. After all, it is much easier to bitch and moan about how bad everything is and to just sit down and be at the mercy of outside forces.

This program is about taking control of just two of the many opportunities that are available to you right now. This book will show you in detail how to create two very distinct and different cash flow machines but how to combine them together to really turbo-charge your income and wealth-building efforts.

Timing is an important factor in almost any business venture or investment and one of the two wealth creators we will discuss is very time-sensitive. The other one has been a wealth creator for thousands of years and yet you probably have never even thought of it in terms of you building wealth for you and your family. The time-sensitive wealth creator is real estate and the unique opportunity that is at your fingertips at this point and time. The truth is, you can make money in real estate during any economy. However, the strategy you use will change dramatically depending on the kind of real estate market you are dealing with at a certain time. I am going to show you a world of cash flow that is open to anyone who has the guts to go out and get their share of it right now. I also think that the opportunity is huge but fleeting for this particular strategy.

The strategy that does not require timing is called *perpetual financing*. Financing it its basic form has been around for about 5,000 years. Yet as old as that strategy is, very few individuals have ever realized that it is one of the most powerful strategies they can use to build THEIR wealth and NOT the bank's wealth. I am talking about you starting your own pool of funds and using that pool as a system to create generational wealth.

Both of these strategies are powerful in their own right and independent of each other, but when combined they are a power-packed income and wealth creator. I am going to show you how to set up your own pool of funds as a financing tool and then use that financing tool to create huge tax-free returns. Have you ever thought of controlling a pool of funds that would be used to create generational wealth? My guess is you have never known you could control a pool of funds and use it for anything you use your local or national bank to do now. Well, after this book and training program, you won't be able to wait to get your financing pool open and funded as soon as possible!

How much money would you have today if you had self financed your purchases with your own financing pool instead of with a traditional bank or finance company? When I teach this material to live classes I have them put their note-taking pens down and add up all the payments they have ever made over their lifetimes. So right now, pick up a pen and calculator or just do the math and add up how much in payments you have paid out over your lifetime. Most people laugh and some even get upset when they actually do the math. The average figure I get from my live classes is about a million dollars in payments over their lifetime. I, of course, get lower and have had much higher and some as high as 20 million dollars worth of payments. Then I will tell them to double whatever that figure is because that is what they would have (or more) if all those payments were growing tax free at a decent interest rate for all those years, while they have been giving their wealth to finance companies and banks. So if the average is $1,000,000 in payments, let's double it to $2,000,000. Now ask yourself this question: "Do I have this amount of money saved for my retirement?" Most people laugh when I ask them that question and say they are nowhere close. That is because we all have been sold a broken business model of putting your income into a 401(k) or some such vehicle and going to the bank and borrowing funds to purchase cars, homes, pleasure items, business equipment, household items, etc. We now hope that our 401(k) invested in the stock market through mutual funds will help us retire, wealthy and with options. In the meantime, during our lifetime we spend millions of dollars in payments to make banks rich and we have almost nothing to show for it. Maybe you might end up with a free and clear house, but most don't, due to constant refinancing or moving and thus returning back to the top of the amortization schedule. So as an alternative to that tried and failed business model, what if we create a financing pool of funds with our money and use that money to close that huge drain of payments going out of our life? If we make similar payments with similar interest rates we paid to the traditional lenders back to our own financing pool could we create a steady wealth creation mechanism? Would that money accumulate no matter what happened in the stock market that day or over a period of years? Could we calculate how much money we would have at a predetermined point of time in our future? The answer to the above is YES!

This book needed to be written to try and help combat the so-called personal financial "gurus" that are all over cable television these days. Most of them still teach the broken business model (make no mistake your family finances are a business) that has made the American public poorer and the banks, finance companies, and Wall Street bankers richer. Well, now it is your turn to build wealth and change your whole financial future for the better. I just saw a show featuring a well-respected financial guru in which she was actually telling people that they may not be able to own a home and that their best days are behind them! It was all I could do not to throw something at my television and cuss her out. She is telling millions of people that their best days are behind them and to hunker down and accept their lot in life as wage earners and follow her "plan" and it will be alright. What a bunch of garbage. First of all she has not a clue what she is talking about when it comes to real estate. The fact is that it is the biggest buyers' market in history and affordability in most areas has not been this low in years. With some specialized knowledge and an action plan you cannot only own your own home but build a cash flow machine that will provide your family with a level of choices that you are wrongly being told are not open to you. That is when I decided to get this message out there to as many people as I could, to show them that their best times are ahead of them and not behind. The fact is, you can have more income, more wealth, more time freedom, and more choices for generations to come. This will require specialized knowledge and training combined with a written action plan to get this implemented. That sounds like it will be hard but it is very easy to get started. It will be easier for you because you will have access to me and my team to make it happen for you and your family.

I don't care what your educational background is or what your work history is because you can succeed with these strategies in spite of them. I am a high school failure and a college dropout but have been able to make an incredible living because I was looking for specialized knowledge. I also knew I wanted to make a lot of money and do it on my own terms. I have spent over $150,000 on seminars, books, home training systems etc. from people who have achieved what I wanted to achieve as well. I was looking for knowledge and most people never really look for knowledge once they get out of school at any level. I have had the good fortune to train thousands of people all over North America who were looking for an edge to create more income and options in their lives. I was able to help many of them start down their own path to having options. I hope you will let me help you and your family as well. Success is not that difficult to attain and really only has a few important steps:

1. Decide what you are good at and what you would like to do to make a lot of money.
2. Find someone who has made a great living doing what you do or something very close to what you believe to be your dream career.
3. Define your niche and what will be your unique selling proposition (USP). In other words, why should people be compelled to do business with you?

4. Match and Model that person and study in depth the systems they use to be successful.

5. Constantly read, listen, and attend training events by people who have achieved more than you in the field you are entering.

6. Develop a marketing plan for your business and commit to testing it for a period of 90 days. Most of these plans can be obtained in the beginning from the experts you will be matching and modeling. You will add your own touch as time goes on.

7. If your marketing is not working as well as you thought, decide if you still feel the product or service is viable and really drill down to your perfect customer and market to only them.

8. When your marketing starts providing good test results, blow out your business by investing on a bigger scale in your marketing.

9. Never quit learning and never give up on being successful. Even if your initial efforts don't succeed as well as you would like, learn your lessons and make it better the next time. Remember, you only fail if you quit trying and working on being successful.

I heard a quote one time that "All men are self-created but only the successful ones admit it." I love that quote because I believe it is so very true. Decide right now to not just read these strategies in this book but to take steps to actually IMPLEMENT THEM! These will be simple to set up and yet life-changing for those who will implement them into their lives.

Now is the absolute perfect time for this book because now is the time you are reading it. This is your time to start down a road to wealth and take advantage of an opportunity that has a brief window of time open to maximize the chance. Don't believe all the pundits that tell you your best times are behind you and there is no opportunity. I am going to train you how to start your own pool of funds and treat them as a financing pool that when done properly will guarantee liquid cash that can be turned into a cash flow machine. I will then train you on some possibilities that are open to you that you may choose to combine with your newly created financing pool to give you the chance to create wealth at an accelerated rate. These two strategies work perfectly together but they do not require each other to be successful. They are great strategies in their own right but when they are combined, the sky is the limit. Not only am I going to train you how to get both set up but my team and I will help you get them both up and running and provide turn-key systems for both to be successful.

So as we close out this opening chapter and get ready to launch into the rest of the book, make yourself a commitment not just to read this book (although that is the first step) but to follow through with the step-by-step instructions at the end of the book. So many good ideas are never acted upon because life gets in the way. So many are so busy making a living that they have no time to make any real money or create real changes. That is their choice to run their lives like that; it is your responsibility to choose to act and not just read. Let's talk about how this book will be different than any other book you have ever read on investing or real estate.

Chapter Two

HOW THIS BOOK WILL BE DIFFERENT THAN ANY OTHER FINANCIAL OR REAL ESTATE BOOK YOU HAVE EVER READ

I just spent three remarkable days with John Jamieson, who was the main lecturer at a seminar in Los Angeles. He is a natural teacher, experienced investor, and for me the whole package... John has hit the top of my Guru Chart... I recommend to all those investors who have been looking like geniuses because of a strong local economy, it's time to listen and get some real methods and ideas from John Jamieson, who knows how to make money in a challenged market.

—Candice Johnson

New business and investing books hit the market every month and many are loaded with good, positive ideas to help you make or keep more money. That is the good news. The bad news is there is so much of the same information just re-taught in a different way by a different author. So if you learn better with repetition (and we all do) maybe those books will help you build wealth. Sometimes however, it is important to have a truly unique approach to investing and building wealth. I know of no other books or training programs on the market that show these unique and simple strategies. The funny thing about that is banks and large corporations all use one of the strategies I am going to share with you and have hundreds of billions of dollars invested in the same way I am going to show you but you have never heard of it UNTIL NOW!

It seems on the surface that we are going to be talking about investing as our main topic which would put us in the same class as 3 million other books past and present talking about markets. We could talk about stocks, bonds, mutual funds, municipal bonds, real estate, and the dozens of other investment vehicles out there.

We are going to talk about real estate investing but not in a way that you have ever seen before. We will not be talking about any other type of investing but rather "financing" as a way to build wealth. We will be talking about reversing money flow out of your life and putting it back into your life. It is the simplest and least known way to build wealth. Leonardo Da Vinci is well known as an absolute genius in several areas and came up with many inventions that have stood the test of time. He was also known for saying some of the best solutions he ever came up with were also the simplest! In other words, it is not always about being creative or innovating but about using what is already there but maybe in just a little different way, creating a huge difference in results.

So, many of us are looking for the latest and greatest way to make money and we sometimes neglect what is right in front of our face. You will feel this way after you are trained by this book. The financing solution to reverse money flow is a huge game changer and will create tremendous wealth for you and your family for generations to come. It is a winner that big corporations, banks, and wealthy people have been using for generations. However, most of the rest of us have been taught the broken business model we talked about in the first chapter. That is about to change for you because you will start treating your personal and business finances in a different way than you have seen before. However, your finances will even be more powerful because you will be smaller and much more nimble than banks or corporations are and thus and have the ability to put your money to work in ways that the above-mentioned institutions cannot.

This book is extremely focused on only two main strategies that are powerful and yet most people have not heard of them and if they have heard of them, they have no idea how to make them work in the real world. You will be loaded for bear when you are done with this book and ready to immediately grow and protect wealth. This will not be complicated theory that will take forever to understand and longer to implement. You will be given step-by-step instructions on how and why to set up your own financing pool of funds and your own real estate money machine. If you choose, this system will be a reality in your life in 4-8 weeks from the time you contact my team. Results, not just information, are the key difference you will receive by reading this book.

Most authors are just that, *authors*, and focus on writing books that sell many copies. They don't really want to work with you personally in their business. So they can afford to talk about theory and strategies that may or may not currently work. Many authors have dropped out of the business world and have gone into the publishing world. I don't think there is anything wrong with that but in doing so they try to build up a wall between them and their readers. I am in the trenches of what I will be teaching you every day and want to help you implement what you will learn here in this book and training program. I will not only teach you, but I will also walk you through step-by-step to get you profitably set up with your own financing program and, if you wish, use that financing program or "pool of funds" if you decide to buy heavy cash flow real estate.

How would you like to be able to take about $25,000 and put it somewhere so that it would generate $6,000 a year in income during the time you owned the property and the potential to double or triple your initial investment in the upcoming years? So if you were in a position to put in $250,000 into the program, you could generate around $60,000 a year in passive repeating income. That income, if set up properly and used in conjunction with your own financing pool, could legally be income tax free! Yes, you could be making that much money and legally paying very little or no income tax on the cash flow. Now, you also have the potential of that initial $250,000 investment to grow to $500,000 to $1,000,000 that you could use for retirement purposes. That is great cash and cash income that can be mostly income tax-free with huge backend growth. That is only a part of this program, but if it was all there was, it would be a fantastic program in and of itself. However, this is only the tip of the iceberg in terms of how good this program will be for you and your family.

You have in your hands the chance to change your financial future with a few simple actions. I also want to address something right now as to whom this book is really for at this time. It is for anyone who has income or assets of any kind. If you are totally broke (financially) at this time, this is not a program you will go out and implement to start to create money from nothing. You absolutely have the power to do that, but it will not be with this training program. If you have zero or very low income and no assets, then you need to get trained on some other strategies to get your income up to a certain level. Have no fear because I started with no money, no job, and no credit and am in the top 1.0% of income earners, so don't get worried about where you are now. Visit my site and program that is designed for people who need to make more money and start to accumulate hard assets. (By the way, you have every asset you need to make a lot of money between your ears if you will just feed it.) Go to my site at www.multipleweatlhstreams.com

and see what I have set up for you to build income quickly. Use those strategies and then implement these two core strategies right away to build and protect wealth.

If you make income and have any kind of assets, pay attention and get ready to implement these strategies right away. You have in your hand the ability to retire early and with much more money than you are currently on pace to have. I used some bigger numbers above but don't panic if you don't have a quarter million dollars to get started. I just needed to use some numbers to get you excited. If you have $5,000 or $5,000,000 or more, we can help. The main thing is to start with what you have and move forward every year. It is not about where you start, it is about where you finish. Most people reading this are making income and many of you are contributing money into qualified plans (401(k)s, IRAs and the like) to help you retire. When you understand what I am telling you, many of you will be rethinking that old business model of qualified plans and opting for the Perpetual Financing™ plan.

This book is about powerful information and simplicity. You'll notice it is not a huge book loaded with all kinds of information that is complicated. It is not about many different topics that you can treat like a smorgasbord and pick and choose what you like. It is not complicated with a lot of theory designed to impress you on how much I know and how little you know.

It is just about laser-focused knowledge that you will use to change your family's future. We will talk about only a few key concepts that all work together to guarantee your creation and protection of wealth.

This is only the beginning of our journey together. If you permit me, I want to forge a lifelong relationship with you that will benefit both of us in the long run. I am not just an author; in fact I don't claim to be a great writer. What I do claim is I am an author who has been in the trenches and actually done what I am writing about in a big way. We are talking about building a real estate and financing money machine and I not only teach it, I have done it for my family and myself. I don't teach theory and things you could do, I teach real world strategies that I have done *and* that I can personally help you do as well.

I know a best-selling real estate author who has sold millions of books on the real estate investment topic. I myself bought a couple of his books and I enjoyed them. However, many of the strategies taught inside of them are generic and border on impossible to accomplish in the real world on any kind of regular schedule. The strategies sound sexy and fill up a lot of pages but they are not real world kind of strategies. This book and training system are designed to be very simple and hands-on so you can generate real wealth and income very quickly. It boils down to be as simple as this:

1. Start your own properly designed financing pool of funds
2. Borrow money from those funds and redirect the money flow in your life to you instead of away from you.
3. Acquire solid cash producing assets (usually real estate) that pumps out money every month just like an own oil well.
4. Pay back your financing pool, which will create a tax-free, wealthy financing pool (which is great since you control the financing pool).
5. Have your financing pool and your real estate money machine pay you for years to come without much involvement from you at all.
6. Grow wealth in several different worlds tax-free and retire early and wealthy.

Those are the simple yet life-changing steps we are going to cover in this book and training system. I have taught 3-day creative financing retreats all over the country to thousands of people but I can teach this in about 3 hours and people are blown away. I know you will be blown away as well but that is not enough. Many people in these retreats do actually act on the information I give them but the majority do nothing with it except take notes and throw the notes in a drawer. What a shame; that is for their family's future. This is another case of knowledge being confused with power. Knowledge is not power but only potential power. Power comes from having SPECIALIZED KNOWLEDGE COMBINED WITH A SPECIFIC ACTION PLAN. So I challenge you to not only complete this book and training system but then to ACT IMMEDIATELY TO BEGIN TO GET IT IMPLEMENTED IN YOUR LIFE. If you won't commit to that, please put the book down now and save yourself the next few hours. This will be a waste of your time without the heart to follow through and implement. Don't let this become like so many training programs: only decoration on your bookshelf. These are the keys to the kingdom, but you must pick the keys up to turn the locks. I will give you the keys and help you turn them to get into the kingdom.

Chapter Three

MARKET MYTHS AND HOW TRADITIONAL FINANCIAL VEHICLES ARE MAKING YOU BROKE

"I could never have achieved what I have today without the help and support of Joe and John. Thanks to their honesty, diligence, and knowledgeable expertise, I was able to purchase several properties, which give me a terrific cash flow, not to mention the capital I have in these lovely homes and the equity I am building up.

I am not from Michigan; I am not even an American. Therefore, I really needed to be able to depend completely on them. They handled everything for me - advised me in which areas to purchase, and which not. They inspected the properties thoroughly. They also handled all the paperwork, the banks, title companies, lawyers, and everyone else involved. Any rehab that was needed, they found the best people to do it at the most reasonable cost, and oversaw it every step of the way. Finally, they found qualified renters for every property. All this in my absence. I could not be more pleased as every decision made was based on solid, well-researched information.

In my position I really needed to find people I could rely on and trust completely - I found them in Joe and John.

Stephanie, Montreal, Canada
An extremely happy Michigan real estate investor

There are so many market and money myths that are not true that we could be here all day discussing them and showing you why they are myths. We are not going to concern ourselves with most of them but we will tackle a few and blow them out of the water.

We discussed in Chapter One how much money you would have today if you could have saved all the payments you paid the banks back inside your own account that was growing at even a small rate of return. This is the first exercise I do with a client when they first come to me for a consultation. I want to make sure you understand that I am not a certified financial planner in any way, shape, or form, nor do I want to be in any way, shape, or form. I am just a student of money and wealth that has made, lost, and made back his own personal fortune. I am an expert at creating multiple six-figure incomes in different arenas simultaneously. This was all started as a high school failure and college dropout. Now that we have made that perfectly clear, let's talk reality.

Banks and Finance companies get stinking, filthy rich off of 97% of people in this country because the finance companies understand and utilize strategies that the average consumer and the vast majority of business people don't understand. The two biggest strategies they know how to use and that you don't are volume of money and the velocity of money to create wealth. While this is occurring, we are taught a broken business model that you see below. That broken business model tells us to do a few things.

1. Take your income and try to save 10% of every dime you make to build a rich retirement. This seems like good advice but we need more than advice, we need strategies that can be easily implemented. As of this writing we have a national savings rate of 2% and that is up from a negative savings rate just a few short years ago.

2. Put that 10% into mutual funds to diversify risk and help the money grow. Most of those funds we are told to invest in the stock market.

3. When you need money for a car, home, business, college, credit cards, etc. just go to the bank (if you have good credit) and they will be happy to loan you the money to purchase these items.

4. Keep your money in the bank in any number of vehicles such as checking, savings, CDs or go to their "registered investment representatives" to invest in other vehicles (mostly stocks and more mutual funds).

5. Borrow at low interest rates and any time you can refinance at a lower rate, do so because your payments will be less, thus putting you in a better financial position in the long run.

6. Put money in a 401(k) or other qualified plans (IRA) and let that be invested long-term, and you will have tax-deferred money over the long run and retire wealthy.

It is hard for me to even write all those steps because I now realize what a bunch of garbage those steps are and how they are keeping us broke. Let's look at each step and look at it another way. Remember most of the people who are telling you to do these things do not have your financial future at the root of their advice. They have their own reasons to advise you to do the steps above and it is almost always money-related. Even the people who truly have your best interests at heart and tell you all about that business model just don't know there is a far better solution. This brainwashing is generations old now and will be hard to overcome. Be your own council on this, just think about it logically, and look at your results so far with your money. If you are happy with them, just continue to do the same things and you will get the same results. If you are not happy with them or know they can and should be better, pay attention.

Myth number 1: "The 10% Solution"

Most people are struggling with their income and can't find enough income to meet their monthly needs. Some of this is caused by poor financial planning and poor financial knowledge but much of it is caused by them paying out way too much in debt payments. The average American pays out about 35% of their income in monthly payments to lending institutions for cars, homes, credit cards, etc. They also pay out around 35 to 40% in federal and state taxes. Now add in basic living expenses and all the sales tax that goes with those purchases. Then tack on fees to do everything both from the government and businesses. Do you see 10% left on the table? Almost never and if there is that much left, now factor in any kind of entertainment or an emergency such as car or medical and there goes your 10% out the door. That is why the national savings rate is pitiful and it is not just because people are not good with their money. Many are doing what they have been educated to do and yet their results are poor. But have no fear as next month will be better won't it? There is a simple solution that we will talk about more as we go deeper into this subject. Just know for now that this broken business model was designed by banks and brokerage companies for their benefit and not yours. Now you can design your own plan that will give you use, focus, and control of your money that will benefit you and your family and not the banks and brokerage houses.

Myth number 2: Mutual funds are the way to wealth

Mutual funds have been touted for decades by every brokerage house, financial planner, and financial guru as the surest and safest way to build wealth. The reason being that most funds (stock funds anyway) invest in a group of stocks and/or sectors of stocks. So the theory goes that you diversify your risk by owning interest in a mutual fund that owns the individual stocks. That way you don't own any one stock and you are diversified. Many people have come to believe that they are somehow free from risk because they are "diversified." That myth was blown out of the water about 4 years ago when the financial crisis caused the stock market to go into free fall mode for a long period of time. Too many investors saw the value of their accounts go down 40 to 70% in just a matter of a couple of months or less. That bath caused some people to realize how vulnerable their retirement was to the whims of the stock market.

Also with mutual funds there can many times be unfavorable tax treatment depending on how they are owned. You could be charged with tax if your mutual fund goes up in value even though you did not sell out. So you could owe tax on money that has not really been realized. It is important that you understand the fortunes created by financial companies who sell and create these funds. The money generated for Wall Street is in the hundreds of billions of dollars annually and it filters down to the sales people on the street. I am not advocating or advising not to be in the stock market or mutual funds. Remember, I am not licensed to advise you on those matters. I can only tell you to understand how this works and don't think for one second that it is the only way to build wealth. I happen to personally believe there are far better and safer ways to create guaranteed wealth for your future.

The vast majority of people have no idea if they are up and down in their 401(k)s or IRAs because they just put in money from each check (those that do contribute) and let it ride. Does it sound like gambling to you? It should. When most people take the time to see how much they have put in their accounts and compare it to what they actually have in their accounts, most are shocked and disappointed. There is no need that you have to be one of them. The key to making your money grow is control and security. If you can maintain much control and do things that are very secure and time-tested, you will be wealthy quickly and almost effortlessly.

I will show you how to take back control over your finances and take the control back from Wall Street. I will show you how to be able to predict wealth easier and with more certainty. Don't think that you are not qualified to handle some of your own money. The truth is that most brokers or financial planners have no clue how to create wealth. Most of them are low to medium income earners and do not practice what they preach. Most of them will not own any of the investments they tell you to own. That seems ridiculous to me and they should be ashamed of themselves for not being in the same arena they are throwing you and your future into.

What I am going to teach you about I not only teach but also have fully participated in and will do so for the rest of my days. I will teach this to my sons and God willing, some day, my grandchildren, and create generational wealth. I have always believed that if you are telling and teaching people how to build wealth you should have your own skin in the game in which you are asking them to play. I believe in setting up cash flow machines through your own financing pools and through strong cash flow real estate. In my opinion there is not a better business model for wealth and cash flow.

I would ask you to consider treating your family finances like a bank or large corporation treats their finances. I will show you what banks do shortly and it is not buy mutual funds! You will learn to create a solid cornerstone of wealth that will last for generations. You will not only know how to do it, but you will have the ability to work with my team to help you get it done.

Myth number 3: Get in the Habit of Using Banks to Finance your Life

If you go out in any area with any sizeable population you see dozens of bank branches during the course of your day. They would like for you to think of them as a friendly neighborhood place where you can come and deposit your money and borrow any funds you might need to live your life. After all, that is how it is done isn't it? For the first 40 years of my life that is what I was taught and that is what I bought into without giving it any thought. I did not really understand how the volume and velocity of money worked and realize now, most of the time those wealth principles were working against me and not for me. The vast majority of you are in the same boat I was in where volume and velocity is working against you. That does not mean that you have not accumulated some assets and have some money in the bank. You may indeed have done well in the money department. However, no matter how well you have done, volume and velocity have cost you another small fortune.

Financing, borrowing, and lending have been around for thousands of years and have created more wealth than any other vehicle on the planet. When you go into every major city in America and for that matter the world, one of the most beautiful buildings in any metropolitan area is a bank. They are usually tall, loaded with tinted glass, oak, brass, marble, and impeccably decorated and furnished. Do you think the banks are building those facilities because they don't understand how money works or wealth is created? Banks and finance companies have been around so long because their business model, when executed properly, is a fantastic business model. You will understand why before we are through with this training.

Banks are not put in place to help you build wealth but to help them and their owners build wealth. Their entire business model is designed to take money out of your pocket and put it in into theirs, and do so rapidly. I can here you saying, "Okay, John, but what can we do about it? After all, they are the bank!" So many people don't understand that they have a choice and if they choose, they can bow out of the banking industry for life. At the very least, they can make the bank an institution that does not have control over anything but a very small part of their family's financial future.

Have you ever thought of controlling your own pool of funds and using it as a financing vehicle? I would wager that most of you have never considered it for more than a fleeting second. I am not talking about a federally charted brick and mortar finance company or bank. I am talking about a vehicle that uses the same principles of wealth creation as lenders have for centuries. You need to understand that a bank is about creating wealth for the bank and its owners. It is up to you to create wealth for your family. The bank is designed to take advantage of two of the most powerful wealth creators in history while at the same time keep us in the dark about how they are picking our pockets, legally and with a smile on their faces!

Those days will be gone for you shortly and you will control your own financing pool or pools that can create long-term and tax-free wealth for generations to come. You will be the one who started this for future generations, so I take this book very seriously and I hope you will as well. Once funded, this financing pool will probably initially fund your family's needs and when the financing pool expands beyond that function, it will fund your business and investment needs. From that point, it will provide funding (if you choose) to other families and businesses. You will have your own financing pool and it can be a huge wealth creator and protector. I am going to show you what banks and large corporations do with their money. Not what they tell us to do with our money because they do not do with their money what they propose that we do with ours. They have a better system and they keep it close to the vest and protect its inner workings with diligence. Most people who work at the bank have no idea how the bank creates wealth. Not even the bank vice presidents and presidents. This kind of knowledge is reserved for the people at the top floors who control the banks. Well now you will know as much as many bank vice presidents about how the bank really makes its money. More importantly than that, you will know how to take those same wealth principles and apply them to your personal and business finances to create a pool of wealth.

Myth number 4: Don't pool your funds and self finance, instead put your money into bank accounts and invest your money in mutual funds. Let the banks worry about the banking process.

You see it all the time when you enter your friendly neighborhood bank. From the moment you enter the entryway there are signs and posters telling you what the bank can do for you. Ask yourself if these slogans sound familiar:

1. Ask us about our low interest rates on a line of credit
2. 60 month CD rates at 2.3%
3. We help finance dreams (pictures of boats, motorcycles, vacation homes, etc.)
4. Need a small business loan?

These and more can be found today at your friendly neighborhood bank. The sales job does not stop there as it only intensifies when you enter the hallowed ropes and go to a bank teller. The following will sound very familiar to you if you either currently, or have at some point in the past, had more than $10,000 in a checking or savings account. Now here is where you get hit up with an offer that will benefit you (not really but it sure sounds good on the surface): "Mr. Jamieson, I noticed you have $30,000 in your checking account, savings account, etc. and that is probably not the best place to put it as you are earning very little, if any, interest. Would you like to sit down with one of our bankers so they can show you how to make much more interest on your money?" A good portion of people say sure or yes they would, but it will have to be another time as they are in a hurry. Now the really aggressive tellers (there are not many but they do exist) are trained to respond, "No problem, Mr. Jamieson, why don't we set up a time next week with your banker, Brian, and you can put it into your book and we will get it done?" Let's assume you do decide to talk to a banker.

The pitch goes one of a few ways depending on how much money you have in that bank. You are told money market for your checking account, CD's for your savings and while we are on the topic, how have your stock market or mutual funds been doing? Well you really need to talk to our registered investment representative Susie Sometime who is a whiz-bang at investments. Now you go into the hallowed office of the registered representative and move your money with us to our "wealth management account" and now we as the bank will get a piece of whatever you do from now until kingdom come. "Does that sound good to you, Mr. Jamieson?" The bank is obviously reasonably successful with this business model and if that does not work, they have a direct mail campaign to continue the assault on your money.

"Now in the meantime, don't worry about major purchases such as cars, boats, homes, or business loans because if you should need those we can take you over to our loan department and get you a new loan for whatever you should need." What I just briefly described has been going on in one form or another for centuries and is rarely questioned by the general public. We just assume this is the way it is and this is what we should do to get ahead with money in our lifetimes. Rubbish, rubbish, rubbish!! There is a far better way that you can control and take all the control out of the bank's hands. Make no mistake; the bank's plan is about their total control and not yours. We need to take back control of our money flow and you will have the tools to do that when you are done with this training system.

Myth number 5: Always be on the lookout for a better rate and refinance anytime you can to save money.

This is my favorite myth to debunk because it has caused so many of us such great harm and we did not even know it! It sounds so financially proper and correct to shop the best rate and refinance anytime you can save a point or two. This philosophy should have made more Americans wealthy over the last 20 years as rates have been coming down for two decades and some people have refinanced everything they own 4 and 5 times and have smaller payments than they did before. So if that's the case, it stands to reason that they are wealthier now than they were before right? Is that the case for you? The overwhelming majority of families who have practiced this old myth are in fact much poorer than they should be! There are a couple reasons for this and they are as follows:

1. Part of this flawed theory is that the lower payment is a good thing because now you can invest the difference between your old and new payments into an investment vehicle and create wealth. Sounds good but almost nobody does that. They in fact just have that extra money flow into their lives and flow it right back out in the form of junk purchases or more loans on other depreciating assets. The alleged savings are really never accounted for and are eaten up with other expenses.

2. The other wealth-stealer that we have not been trained on is the actual interest "volume" of the loan and not just the interest "rate." It stands to reason that you would prefer to have a 5%

rate as opposed to a 7% rate but that is not the only question you need to ask when determining financing any purchase. If you refinance to get that lower payment, how many years are you adding on your total pay-off and payment schedule? An example: We currently have a $100,000 mortgage balance on our home and we are paying 7% on a 30 year loan that we have been paying on for 12 years. So if we continue to make our payments as scheduled, we will pay off in 18 years. But now we have the opportunity to refinance our loan and get the interest rate down to 5.5% thus lowering the monthly payment. However, the trade-off is now we start back to the top of the amortization schedule and went from 18 years worth of payments back to 30 years worth of payments. The bank took a loan that was actually starting to pay off the principle instead of being all interest and turned it back into a loan that is heavily loaded with front-end interest thus increasing their interest volume dramatically. What is interest volume? Very simply put, how much of your payment is going to interest (bank's profit) and how much is going toward the debt pay down (your money)? In the beginning years of a 30-year mortgage your interest volume is a staggering 90%! So you just refinanced (which cost you money in costs as well) and agreed to pay the bank for your lifetime and into your children's lifetimes as well. People have done that a half dozen times on several loans from houses to cars to boats to investment real estate and every other loan under the sun. We should all be richer but almost none of us are. Who is richer for it? You guessed it, you friendly neighborhood bank.

You have to start thinking about the bank as the mafia when it comes to money lending. They both would like to "juice" you over a long period of time and have you paying a ton of interest before you ever pay back the principle. The banks' rates are better and their collection process is healthier (most of the time) but the wealth concept is the same for both institutions. The longer they can have you making payments, the better off they are and the broker you become.

As I get older and I look at people that are financially secure in their older years, they have several things in common, but one of the biggest common traits is they have no debt. Their homes are owned free and clear, (I know many investment advisors will tell you that a free and clear home is a terrible waste of your capital and you should have a mortgage and invest the monies into the market. I have come to believe that is really bad advice for reasons we will discuss in a later chapter) their cars are paid for, they have no credit card debt, and they have stable, reliable income from a source that does not require them to work to have the income come in every month. Most of the people I just described are not stinking, filthy rich but are very comfortable, have options to travel as they please, and have very little worries about money. Payments to lending institutions are a drain on your wealth and should be eliminated as soon as possible. That money should be immediately reversed back into your life and create wealth for you and your family. That is what we do for our clients and what we will do for you. We will simply get out of your way and you will grab a hold of a huge wealth creator that has been in front of your face for years.

Myth number 6: Invest your money into 401(k)s and other qualified plans

Financial gurus have been telling people for years that the key to wealth is to take at least 10% of your income and invest it into a 401(k) or some other tax deferred qualified plan. This is another myth that sounds so good on the surface. Let me state again I am not a certified financial planner nor do I want to be a financial planner. I am only going to point out some downfalls with this strategy and give you some other alternatives you should explore. One of the things you always want to study when it comes to money is what do wealthy people and businesses do with their money to create wealth. Rich people, corporations, banks, and insurance companies control most of the wealth in the country so, why don't we study what they do with their funds? Studying wealth to become wealthy has always made sense to me. So with that thought in mind, do rich people and the other groups put their money into 401(k)s or other qualified plans? The answer is no, for a couple reasons. The first reason is they don't even qualify to have one of those plans most of the time. When they do qualify, most do not participate because they realize it is not their best option. Wealthy people and companies do other things with their money, which we will discuss in an upcoming chapter.

Qualified plans have been touted as the best wealth-builder when combined with mutual funds. Most qualified plans invest in stock mutual funds, which are pooled money that then buys individual stocks on behalf of the fund. As one of the fund investors, you own a portion of the fund, which in turn owns the stocks, and if the stocks perform well, you make money, and if they don't, you lose money. The fact that you own them inside of your 401(k) makes any potential profits tax-deferred. Some 401(k)s offer matching from an employer, which can be attractive, as it is free money that gets put into your account. The idea behind a mutual fund is your investment is diversified because you don't actually own the individual stock, you own a group of stocks. Most funds invest in a similar "sector" such as technology, retail, or biotech, etc. If you have more than one fund (as many people do), those different funds are supposed to give you an even more diversified portfolio against risk of loss. Do you think it is a good bet that your different funds own many of the same stocks? I have spoken with people that had taken the time to look at the true holdings of their funds and most found out the funds owned many of the same stocks even though they were different funds with different companies! You think you are so "diversified" that you can't figure out when the market goes south how come you are losing so much money in each fund? The answer is because so many of the different funds own the same stock or the same sector of stocks. So when Microsoft (just for an example) goes through a downtime in their stock price, many tech companies follow in sympathy. You had no idea that you owned Microsoft or other related companies in several different funds.

The brief explanation above is not meant to be the end of your education when it comes to 401(k)s, IRAs, or mutual funds but a mere starting point. When we discuss other options we will compare them to qualified plans so it is important that you have a basic understanding of qualified plans. In short, a qualified plan is a plan approved by the IRS that enables you to invest pre-tax or post-tax dollars (depending on the plan) and that money is usually invested in mutual funds (although it does not have to be) on a tax-advantaged basis. Many people believed that their funds were protected from any serious downturns due to the "diversification" aspect of mutual funds. The financial collapse of 2008 reminded them of the inherent risk of having significant monies in the stock market even if it is through a mutual fund. Many people saw their accounts lose 40-70% of their values and many have still not rebounded several years later. One of the biggest wealth-stealers for most people is the loss of capital or principle in market losses. If you put money in the market and it drops 50%, that means from that point on your money has to double just to get back to even. If you can have a system that protects your principle and assures you can't go backwards, you will be way ahead of the curve by protecting your principle. Many people make the mistake of having most or all of their net worth and retirement plans in the stock market and hoping it works out. You must understand that hope is not a plan. You must have a plan for wealth creation and retirement that is not so dependent on the stock market performing. Don't believe the myth of average rates of return and the old adage of just riding it out and staying in it until it turns around. That is antiquated thinking and is only for people who don't know about other options. There are many more options available for you to truly diversify your wealth and provide a great retirement. You will have some of the most powerful tools for wealth creation available when you are done with this book and training program.

Chapter Four

THE BROKEN FINANCIAL MODEL WE HAVE BEEN SOLD AND WHY 99% OF AMERICANS ARE GETTING ROBBED

Hello, my name is Mike Biglane and I have been a personal one-on-one mentor for real estate investors all over the country and have done over 100 personal mentorships. I have worked with John at trainings where he was the main trainer and I was the mentor and sales associate. I am impressed with John not only as a speaker and trainer but also with his vast knowledge of real estate and business. John is one of the few speakers I have met that I consider qualified to do in the field mentoring. John is very knowledgeable about wealth creation and preservation.

After the first time we worked together, I immediately requested that anytime they could put me on an event with John, I wanted the opportunity to work with him at other events. I have been involved with over ten thousand real estate closings as an owner of a title company in Florida. There are very few people I have ever met in the real estate industry that know it any better than John knows the business.

I have no doubt that you will be pleased that you have John on your side in helping you build your own family fortune through perpetual financing, real estate, and private lending.

Best Wishes,
Mike Biglane
National Real Estate Mentor

We have already briefly discussed the broken business model in a previous chapter. The broken business model is summed up below.

1. Try to put 10% of your income into mutual funds for retirement.
2. Keep the rest of your money in the bank or with their investment advisors.
3. Borrow money from the bank for your big purchases and investments and pay them interest over the next many years. The average American pays out 35% of their income in payments to lending institutions.
4. Pay no real attention to the total cost of your payments and outgoing cash flow but pay attention to the "rates of return" you earn on your investments.

Do you see anything wrong with those numbers? We try to save 10% of our income (I say *try* because the national savings rate is less than 2% and that is up from negative savings a few short years ago) while at the same time we shell out 35% of our money back to banks, which includes mostly front end loaded interest. We are constantly searching for those illusive double-digit rates of return while at the same time we are losing more than that every month in payments to the banks. Please review the diagram below to see how this looks.

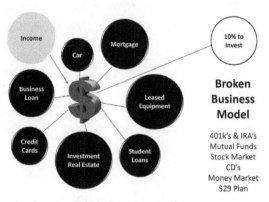

Broken Business Model

401k's & IRA's
Mutual Funds
Stock Market
CD's
Money Market
529 Plan

35% of your income gone to payments for life!

We, as investors and businesspeople, are always searching for the latest and greatest way to get ahead and make more money. Meanwhile, we have a boatload of money leaving our lives every month that we will mostly never see again in our lifetimes. So here is a radical idea: what if we simply redirect that money flow back into our lives and we keep the money that we are currently giving to banks and finance companies?

Do this simple exercise again to hammer home the point of cash flow over your lifetime and how you are making banks rich and keeping yourself broke, or if not broke, certainly with far less than you should have. Add up all the payments you have made in your lifetime on cars, real estate, credit cards, student loans, business loans, equipment, and any other thing you can think of off the top of your head. Now whatever that figure is… double it! Why? Because you must accept in your heart that money is either earning you interest or you are losing interest you should have gotten because you made a payment to some else's bank instead of a financing pool you own. In short, interest does not sleep. You either are earning it or losing out on it. So if your lifetime payment figure was $1,000,000 then double it because that is at least how much you would have if that $1,000,000 would have been put into an account that you control. What if you would have just gotten 6% interest on the money; could that $1,000,000 have turned easily into to $2,000,000? Now add up all the money you have saved for retirement or your later years if you never retire. Are your funds saved even close to the payments you have made over the same time frame you have been making payments? If they are, congratulations, you are the first person who has ever said yes in the thousands of people I have taught these concepts to all over the country. Most people belly laugh when they see the difference between how much the banks have of their money and how much they have of their money.

It is time to stop the madness and redirect that money flow into your own financing pool that is designed to compound tax-free for generations to come. It is time to take the power back from the banks and give it back to you and your family. It really is as easy as making the decision to redirect your money flow and to implement a proven system for doing so and taking back control of your financial future.

This next diagram shows what a new better personal and business model might look like after it is set up for you. Notice you have closed the circle of wealth in your life and money begins to pool quickly and seemingly effortlessly.

Perpetual Financing Wealth System
Reverse Your Money Flow

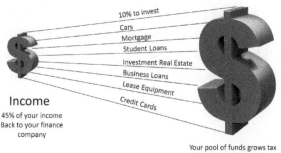

10% to invest
Cars
Mortgage
Student Loans
Investment Real Estate
Business Loans
Lease Equipment
Credit Cards

Income
45% of your income
Back to your finance
company

Your pool of funds grows tax free. Access anytime without penalty. Guaranteed strong growth, withdraw tax free!

Please don't think you are alone in getting fleeced by banks and investment houses, because they have been doing it by the hundreds of millions for centuries. This fleecing is not just limited to family finances but also extends to most small and medium sized businesses. Most of them do the same silly things we do as individuals because they are run by individuals who have been given the same broken business model above and follow it without question. So how would they be able to run a company any other way? Most businesses put their money into checking accounts, savings accounts, CDs, and the stock market through mutual funds. They then borrow most of their working capital from banks to buy or lease equipment, office space, expansion of the business, etc. Their net assets never even come close to how much they pay out in payments over the business lifetime. Even moneymaking, successful businesses are giving away fortunes without even realizing it or giving it much thought. After all, don't we have to do it this way? Don't the banks have total control? The answer is an absolute NO!

The truth is we can change this business model starting tomorrow, redirect that money flow, and pick up volume and velocity on our own money. We can also loan that money out to others and pick up volume and velocity on other people's money. There has never been a better time to do this. There is also a huge opportunity to use your own bank's funds to buy income-producing assets like little cash flow properties and make your own fortune that can last for generations to come. Not only will I show you how to do this, my team and I can personally help you achieve these results. You have the proven system in your hands and the ability to tap into a company that can help you every step of the way.

Chapter Five

IT'S THE DIRECTION OF THE MONEY, STUPID!

Wealth Tip and Free Resource: We have a free audio download available at our site. I would like you to have a free audio download on how to sell and make a strong six-figure income. If you don't know how to sell, it will be very difficult to get ahead financially. I was fortunate to learn how to sell early in my life and would like to help you be better at sales. Great salespeople are not born, they are trained. Just visit us online at <u>www.perpetualfinancingsystem.com/selling</u> for your free download.

Yes this chapter is all about something so simple you would think we would not have to be taught it in this day and age. Weren't we all taught about money flow and volume and velocity in grammar school? How about junior high school? How about high school? Well all of us would have learned about it in college, especially business majors. You would think that somewhere along the line we would have been taught these two important wealth principles, but you would be dead wrong in most circumstances. Why weren't we taught it by our teachers? That answer is very simple: they did not know anything about it, nor does 99% of the American public. People can't teach what they don't know themselves. Now most business majors may have been taught one or both of those principles in their undergraduate or graduate level programs. If they were taught those words and what they meant it was done out of a textbook and to make the professor and or author of the textbook sound sophisticated and to impress the class. I can almost guarantee that it was never taught in this format which is very simple and, more importantly, how to use those words to build real guaranteed wealth for your family and provide you with a future most people only dream about.

We have mentioned the term "interest volume" briefly in another chapter but let's dive a little deeper into that and another powerful wealth creator most people have never heard of, the "velocity of money". Interest volume, as we have said, is how much of your payments goes toward interest to the bank and how much goes towards actual owning of the asset or principle pay down. The bank would prefer very high interest volume and you as the consumer would prefer low interest volume. However, if you owned the pool of money collecting interest, would you mind if you were paying high interest volume? If you are picking up the interest volume and it is compounding for you tax-free, would you mind if the interest volume were high? Stop thinking like a consumer and start thinking like a businessperson. Wise businesspeople build fortunes for themselves and their companies. Consumers ALSO earn fortunes for wise businesspeople, but die broke and leave very little, if any, behind for future generations, charities, or foundations. Enough of being Joe or Susie Consumer and on to being Joe or Susie Wealth Attractor!

Why is it that when you borrow $100,000 from a bank on a 30-year mortgage you end up paying back about 3 times that amount? The mortgage amortization always favors the bank and will rob you blind if you don't find a way to cut it back to favor you more. You will know how to do that shortly. Most of us have heard how much we really pay back on a 30-year loan as it usually pointed out to us at the closing table by the closing rep for the Title Company or attorney. It is on the the truth in lending form where it totals your payment. I have been at many hundreds of closings where that figure was pointed out and the reaction almost 100% of the time, is laughter, and people just wanted to ignore it. The fact is that you should not ignore it but study it and decide to cut it down and redirect the money flow to your pool of funds and not to the friendly neighborhood banks pool of funds. Make yourself rich and stop making the banks richer. The banks will always make fortunes because you are one of a tiny fraction of people who will actually take the time to study this and find out how money truly works. Let the banks be wealthy but not on your dime. Time to start thinking like them and acting like them and let your family and friends (who won't listen even when you tell them better) continue to make the lending institutions wealthy.

When you do pay back a traditional bank with all that interest volume what do they do with a good portion of it? Do they let it sit in their vault and count it? Do they roll around naked in it? (If they do I would prefer not to know about it.) Or do they relend the money out again? The answer is, of course, the latter. They loan out the money again and this brings us to a huge principle of wealth called "velocity." I should point out that velocity is not just a wealth principle when it comes to money or banking. It is one of the best producing and least known business principles. It is very simply: the speed at which money or a product can be sold and how many times in a day, week, month, or year that same asset can be sold again and again. Think of a huge company with tons of products to sell, such as Wal-Mart™, Target™, or some other such retailer. Think of a simple bar of soap that this company has bought wholesale from a distributor for let's just say a dollar. Now they have one dollar of theirs tied up into that bar of soap that they now need to sell. When they sell it, lets say they can sell it for $1.50 and create a 50% gross profit on that bar of soap. That is just 50 cents of profit so how do they create billions of dollars on that and other products? The answer is velocity of their products and therefore their money. If they can sell at one store 200 bars of soap a day, they have turned their $200.00 into $300.00 on one product in one day. Now multiply that by thousands of products and similar mark-ups and now you have some real money. Now how does the math change if they can sell them faster? The profit margin is the same but now let's say they sell 300 bars of soap instead of 200 bars of soap? Now they are taking $300 dollars and turning it into $450.00 in one day on one product.

Now think about how they are able to compound this by taking their profit of $100.00 to $150.00 and buying more profitable products and using the velocity wealth principle to expand their wealth. Do you see how this starts to compound with bars of soap or any other product they have on the shelves? Also, the reverse is true; time is an enemy of a retail store. Every day their inventory sits there unsold, that means their dollar is sitting there losing value and not being an asset. They must use velocity to keep the massive money machine rolling. Thanks for the retail lesson, John, but I am not in retail and I thought we were talking about banks and volume and velocity.

This is true but I just described exactly how it works with banks, but *their* main product (but not only product) is money. So the bank owners look to see how many times they can rotate money in and out of their bank. The banks have it even better than the retailers, as they don't even have to spend their own money on the soap in our last example. The soap is money and you and the rest of the

American public are always happy to put money in the bank in one form or another and allow them to use your money as if it is their own inventory so they can loan it out and make outrageous returns for the lending institutions. You see, when the bank makes volume and velocity on their funds, most of the time it is on your funds not theirs! Talk about leverage at its finest. We put our funds on deposit, they take our funds and loan them out to the public at higher rates and make the spread. Then they take the payments and loan them out again and again and again which magnifies their returns. Did you know that many banks of all different sizes routinely make over 100% on their net assets? They are doing this even when the interest rates are at historic lows. Please understand that the bank owners care much more about interest volume and velocity than the actual interest rate. You see, they are going to make a spread no matter what. So if rates are currently at 4% to borrow then they are only going to pay you 1% or less on your deposits and they pick up the difference. If rates go to 13% to borrow money then they will raise their rates, and they'll pay out to around 10% so their spread is about the same.

Now if they can get you borrowing fresh money and refinancing old debt, and keep that interest volume maximized, they are on their way to a great year. At the same time that is happening, they are taking those payments and loaning that money out again, creating more money and profits, and it goes on and on. Is it any wonder why a lending and borrowing system has been around for about 5,000 years in some form or another? I am not out to beat up on banks. On the contrary, I am showing you how to run a profitable money business. I am showing you how to use money as a tool just like they have done for centuries. If you will do that and use the strategies in this training program, you can create generational wealth for you and your family.

Let me give you a brief simple example of the power of velocity of money that was shared with me when I was learning this system several years ago. It shows what banks can do to grow their wealth. If the banks can do this, then so can you in your own personal and business lives.

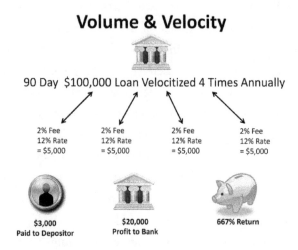

The example starts out as in the diagram above, with you depositing into your local bank $100,000 and being paid a 3% rate on an annual basis on your $100,000. Now the bank takes your money and loans it out as if were their own to a small business owner on a 90 day note. The business owner has to put up collateral, insurance of several kinds, and their business itself for collateral on this loan. All of this transfers risk away from the bank to others, which magnifies the chances of this being a successful loan for the bank. The bank loans the money out with 3 points up front or on the back of the loan (a point is 1% of the loan amount) and let's say 12% for a commercial loan. The business owner must pay the 100k back in 90 days plus $5,000 in points and interest. Now if that were it for the year it would be a good return for the bank but are they just going to sit on that money? No, the more they sit on it, the less valuable it becomes. Remember the term 'velocity' from above? They will take the $100,000 and loan it out again (to say nothing of the $5,000 profit on the loan) and repeat that process as many times as possible.

The illustration shows them loaning that money out 4 times, generating $20,000 in profit on the $100,000, which looks like it is a 20% return on their money which is very attractive to most people. This is the part where I have some fun with my live audiences and ask them what the rate of return is on this scenario and they happily say 20%. The real rate of return is in fact much more than the paltry 20%. Remember the $100,000 the bank is loaning out to the business owner is in effect your money. Now really how it works is once your deposit is made into the bank, they take control of it but must make it available to you at any time (depending on the type of deposit) so they can actually say it is their money but we all know how it really works now. When you realize that the bank is just the clearinghouse for your money you start to realize that you can loan out your own money. The loans will first be loaned out to you so you can change the money flow from making the banks rich to making yourself rich. There will also come a time when you will be loaning out the money to the public for things like real estate, small business loans, and many other things that you are not currently exploring. Now that rate of return goes up to the bank to 667%! The bank only has to pay you $3,000 in interest for the year of using your money and they generated $20,000 profit in this example. Now that is wealth creation at its finest!

I don't want to mislead you into thinking that banks routinely make those kind of returns because they don't, but they consistently hit triple digit rates of return on their net invested assets. No need to take my work for it, please visit a website called www.bauerfinancial.com and do your own research on all kinds of banks and the rates of return they can achieve using volume, velocity, costs, and fees. You can adopt many of the same wealth principles and start to build wealth for now and for generations to come.

Chapter Six

BUILD YOUR OWN PERPETUAL FINANCING SYSTEM FOR GENERATIONAL WEALTH

As a national professional speaker, I always thought I was an outside-the-box thinker when it came to marketing my business dealings. What a treat and literal paradigm shift when John and I had the chance to work together. I was coached by the master himself!

—Dennis Dinoia, National Trainer

So now that we are starting to understand why banking and financing is such a wealth creator or wealth stealer (depending on what side of the table you are on) we now need to talk about how to control a pool of funds that will be used for financing purposes. We need to think like a business owner and not just the consumer. We need to now go through some simple steps on how to create your own pool of money to use as a financing system. There are so many benefits to controlling a financing pool. We need to discuss them fully.

Have you ever heard the theory that banks will only loan money to you when you don't really need it? In other words, if your credit is good, income is stable, and you are going through good times, you can usually get a loan. If you are on the other side of the coin with bad credit, spotty income, and going through some short-term tough times, good luck getting a loan. Well when you control the financing pool, you get your loan without a job, credit, or any other thing valued by traditional lenders. With this Perpetual Finance System, you get your loan with one phone call or one fax in 24 hours. This loan comes at a very low interest rate even during historically high interest times. The loan comes to you without having to qualify at all and for any reason you wish. Create your own financing pool either all at once or over time, but create it as soon as you can. Many people want to know how to create this pool of money or where to store the pool once created. The whole next chapter will discuss this in detail so sit tight and read on as to why we need our own pool of money.

Think of never having to go to the bank for anything again and what power that would give you and your family. Many of you actually have the resources to make that a reality in the next 30 to 60 days. For others of you, who do not have sufficient resources yet to set up your own financing pool, fear not because you can set your financing pool up over time. It will require patience and persistence, but it will be worth your time and effort. After this training is completed, you may start to ask yourself some much-needed questions about contributing to qualified plans and may start redirecting some of your cash flow into the vehicle discussed in the next chapter. A little bit of money adds up over time and you can start a pool of money by focusing your money into a superior vehicle and begin to use volume and velocity starting on a smaller scale and grow it to a larger vehicle in a short period of time.

We will be comparing the benefits of qualified plans and perpetual financing in an upcoming chapter. You be the judge as to the best place to park money and watch it grow after you review the facts.

If you are convinced that starting your own pool of wealth and combining that pool with the wealth principles of volume and velocity is the way to go for long term wealth and security, than we need to determine how to best accomplish this goal. You are going to need to fund your financing pool either with a big opening funding, funding over time, or both. All of these methods are acceptable and will depend on your current economic status and access to resources. No matter which method is best for you, the next question I receive from people goes something like this: "Okay John, I am ready to get this started but where do I put this money to use like a financing vehicle?" The best place to get this started is inside of a properly designed whole life insurance policy. Yes whole life insurance is where you have been told never to put money by the television "gurus". No this is not just plain Jane whole life, as it will have to be structured properly to use it as a financing pool. If you have an old traditional policy, 98% of them will not be structured for financing and money flow. Many of you have whole life policies that are built for insurance purposes but if you have cash value you can borrow it out if you need it. That is not even close to what we are talking about in this training. Make sure you do not close your mind as I did when I was first exposed to this concept. When I heard whole life insurance I thought, "what are you talking about?" I have always been taught that you never put any money inside whole life insurance policies because they are lousy investments. Does that sound familiar to you? When I was getting my initial financial training over 20 years ago that is what every guru told me back then so I took it as gospel truth. The truth is that the guru did not know about how a properly designed life insurance policy works and builds wealth. So I and millions of others were taught that you never buy whole life. The gurus said if you want life insurance you should "buy term and invest the difference" because whole life was too expensive and a bad place to put money. So for over 20 years that is what I thought, and that is how I lived my life. I closed my mind to the thought that those gurus could have been wrong. Things have not changed much in over 20 years except for the names of the gurus on television who keep touting the same message that has been going on for years. That message is very wrong and dangerous but you will never hear anything else from them as they have been wrong for too long and it would take a real person of character to admit they have been wrong. To be fair, if you are talking about dumping money into a whole life insurance policy the way they are normally written then the gurus, both then and now, are correct. That *would* be a lousy place to put money.

However, what they don't know because they have never taken the time to learn is that there are different ways to build a life insurance contract that produces great results and about a dozen benefits that don't exist in any other financial vehicle. So I am going to ask you not to let the gurus of your day, who continue the old "buy term and invest the difference" line, turn you off to one of the greatest wealth creators and wealth protectors of all time. Listen to this training program and read this material and you be the judge. If I can be reprogrammed from being brainwashed, then so can you, if you choose. Start by asking yourself this question: if whole life insurance is such a bad place to put money, then why do major world banks and major world corporations put a good portion of their resources into life insurance contracts? Oh you did not know that they did that, did you? Well if you didn't, you need to know what wealthy institutions and wealthy people do with their money. The first clue is they put very little of it in the stock market and mutual funds. They also don't contribute to qualified plans to build wealth.

Look at the illustration below to see how much major banks have in whole life cash value life insurance. As you can see, Bank of America had just about 16 billion worth of cash value life insurance. The banks and corporations use their policies a little different than you or I will but do you think Bank of America and many other top banks and corporations would be putting tens of billions of dollars into polices if it did not make economic sense? Money is drawn to money and if you want to study wealth, study what wealthy companies and individuals do and not what average or broke people and companies do with their money. That makes sense, so follow the money flow, do what successful companies do, and greatly increase your family's wealth and financial future.

Where does Money put Money?

☐ Bank of America $17 Billion in High Cash Value Life Insurance

☐ J.P. Morgan Chase $12 Billion in High Cash Value Life Insurance

☐ Wells Fargo $7 Billion in High Cash Value Life Insurance

☐ U.S. Bank $6 Billion in High Cash Value Life Insurance

According to Federal Financial Institutions Examinations Council (2008)

We need to understand how a properly designed policy works and all the benefits associated with using one as a financing vehicle.

Chapter Seven

THIS IS NOT YOUR FATHER'S
LIFE INSURANCE POLICY

Wealth Tip: The world of company-sponsored pension plans is going the way of the 8-track player and is almost nonexistent in any new companies. There is, however, a whole world called private pensions that successful business owners use quietly to build a massive wealth stream. This is a secretive world that we have access to and can help to build your own perpetual pension plan. If you or anyone you know has a successful business, this is a must-hear. Before you continue to sponsor that 401(k) or other similar plan, you owe it to yourself to find out more about private pensions. For a free audio track with further explanation please visit www.perpetualfinancingsystem.com/privatepension to get your download.

So why have most of us never been told about the power of a properly built whole life insurance policy designed for use as a Perpetual Financing Vehicle? There are actually a few reasons that come to mind and one of them is the actual insurance industries approach to life insurance. Before we tackle that subject let's talk about the biggest reason: Wall Street! The country and even the civilized world have been taught for about a century now that stocks are where to put your money. We have also been told that stocks have created more wealth than any other vehicle and other things that are just not quite true. You see, there is a ton of money being made by people at all levels of Wall Street and collaborators with Wall Street such as the US government and the corporations whose stock is issued and traded every day on Wall Street and other places. If people move a portion of their wealth away from stocks, then Wall Street perceives this as a bad thing because the powers that be believe that if they don't get all of your money invested in the market, it is a bad thing. I just did a quick Google search and simply put in investing in stocks and got over 46,000,000 hits. I then did a Google search on investing in life insurance and got about 16,000,000 hits on my query. Almost triple the amount of interest in Wall Street as opposed to life insurance. This tells us that people are much more interested in hearing about stocks because that is the way we all have been trained. We are told that stocks are the way to wealth and that the market has averaged (pick a figure) over the last (pick a time frame) and so it will continue to do the same. It is important for you to understand that "average rates of return" can be manipulated and that whatever figure you get from Wall Street does not mean that your money will average that growth rate. Remember this example well: over 4 years, how is it possible to invest $100,000 on year one and average a 25% rate of return for four years and have less than $100,000 after year four and have never taken a dime out of the account during that time? The answer is so easy once you understand how this works. 100k into the account and it grows at 100% year one so now it is worth $200,000. Year 2, the account falls by 50% putting the value back down at 100k. Year 3, the account grows by another 100% and the money is back up to 200k. Year 4, the account dips back down another 50% and our money is now back to 100k. Now you take out taxes you made on the good years (the way mutual fund taxes work is you can owe tax even though you have not sold the asset) and fees, and time value of money and your account is worth quite a bit less than the 100k your started your investment plan out with four years before. Now take a look at your "average rate of return" and you will notice that if you add up 100% return years twice and subtract out your 50% years twice, that leaves you with 100%. You must divide that by the 4-year cycle and what do you get? Of course, I am a high school failure and college dropout but it looks like a 25% "average rate of return." Did your money grow by 25% a year? Not hardly! So be very careful of average rates of return and focus on growth, not rates of return. Focus on cash flow in and cash flow out. Don't get sucked into the age-old trap of just thinking about rates of return. Many times they are put in place so you

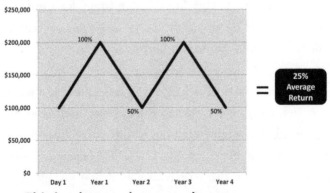

Stop Focusing on Rate of Return

This is what can happen when you give up control of your money.

will take your eye off the ball of what is really happening. What is really happening is that while we are all focusing on rates of return and the rise and fall of the stock market, we are happily pouring our wealth out month after month to the banks and finance companies. Do yourself a favor and write down that figure from the previous exercise about how much you have paid out in payments. Then put it in a place you can see every day to remind yourself that you must reverse that money flow as soon as possible.

Another reason few people think about life insurance as a wealth-building vehicle is that both our parents and most of us still today are sold life insurance based on a needs analysis or income replacement of the client. In other words, it goes like this: Mr. Smith makes $100,000 annual income and has obligations such as a mortgage, car notes, insurance, etc. If he dies tomorrow, how much income will his family lose over the next x number of years? Now find out how much you would have to have invested at 5 or 6% to replace that much income. Once you have that figure you set the policy death benefit for that amount and then determine the cheapest way to make that happen. So Mr. Smith has not been taught the living benefits of a properly designed whole life insurance contract but only the pure insurance portion of replacing income and paying off obligations for the family. Life insurance is looked upon and treated by the insurance representative and client as a pure expense and both look for ways to "save money" on the premium.

That description is what happens in homes and insurance offices all over the country every day. So the industry itself is to blame for most people not understanding the wealth possibilities of whole life insurance when it is done properly. One of the biggest misconceptions about life insurance is that term is cheaper than whole life. That is one of those statements in the same league as a 25% average rate of return. Yes it is true… and it is a bold faced lie at the same time.

The facts are that, as a pure insurance vehicle, term is cheaper than whole life in the initial years, but gets exponentially more expensive as time moves forward. Term insurance is just as it sounds; it is insurance coverage for a set period of time. Usually a 10 to 20 year period or annual renewable term insurance is the most common term insurance vehicle. Let me begin by saying this book is not designed to be the be all and end all for life insurance. There are certainly more in-depth books on this topic. This section is just designed to give some basic information that everyone can understand about insurance policies and their benefits and downfalls. Remember I am a high school failure and college dropout so I like to keep things very simple and relatable. Now back to term insurance in its simplest form. It is a very inexpensive way to provide insurance coverage in the event of a person's death. There is no wealth component, living benefits, or "cash value" to term insurance. The premium is based on age and health, like all life insurance policies. The premium is typically locked in for a period of years, such as 20 years. Then, after that 20 year term is up, the coverage expires and if you want another policy you must either take out another 10 or 20 year policy based on your attained age (if you qualify medically) or you can start to pay annual, renewable term rates that go up every year very dramatically when you are a little older.

Many studies show that only about 2 to 3% of term polices are ever collected on by the beneficiary. That is of course what the life insurance company is betting on when they issue the policy. However, if you are one of the small percentages that gets paid out, your family is certainly glad you had the foresight to protect them with a policy. The theory of term insurance is that you will only need it for 20 years or so because by that time you will have accumulated enough wealth that your family should be protected in the event of your death. What a load of garbage that has proven to be over the last 20 years for the average American family. With many qualified plan accounts down and real estate values dramatically down, many Americans find they are poorer today than they were 20 years ago. Many will never recover that wealth in the next 20 years and if something happens to them before they have a chance to recover, their families will be faced with hard financial times.

Whole life works differently than term insurance and has way more benefits than just insurance. There are many living benefits of a properly designed whole life policy that the life insurance community as a whole does a terrible job of explaining a fraction of the benefits. Most traditional life insurance agents do not truly understand all the wealth-building possibilities they have in front of them for their clients. They believe mostly what consumers believe: that term is cheaper than whole life, so they sell a lot of term. Term is only less expensive on a pure insurance basis in the early years of the policy. Whole life locks in your premium at your current age and it is whole life because you can keep it your whole life once it is in place. Once you qualify for it, the premium is locked in and so is your insurability. So if 10 years from now your physical condition changes, your policy cannot be cancelled or altered assuming you make timely premium payments. There is not "term of insurability" as with term insurance so the policy stays with you your entire lifetime. Most people die between 70 and 90 years old with, of course, exceptions to that rule. That is the time when you will be leaving behind your wealth for your family; your cost of a term insurance policy will be tens of thousands of dollars per year. I had a guest at one of my live trainings one time who was 70 years old and his insurance policy just reset to annual renewable term insurance. His annual premium just for the insurance was almost $70,000 and that was just for the insurance. There was no cash value with that amount; just the insurance policy itself was $70,000. Had he kept his whole life policy the cost of that policy would only have been about $4,000 that year. This was a man who had lost much of his net worth in the economic collapse of a few years before and if he died tomorrow, was not going to leave much behind for his family. How do you think he felt about the buy term and invest the difference philosophy? He is not alone. That same scenario has happened to millions of Americans over the last few years. If a good insurance agent had known how to show them the wealth power of using a whole life policy as a perpetual financing vehicle, they would have much more money than they have today and be assured of leaving behind wealth after their death, income tax free. See if this sounds similar to what you have heard from a life insurance agent at some time in the past. "Okay Mr. Smith, we determined you need $750,000 in insurance to protect your family in the event of your death. Now, if you buy a term insurance policy, it will cost you $900.00 per year to put that policy in place. If you would like to do whole life, it will cost you $3,500 per year, but eventually you will have cash value you can borrow against, should you need the money. Which plan would you like to go with, Mr. Smith?" Which plan looks better to you based on that explanation? So why do many of my clients put hundreds of thousands of dollars into polices in the first couple of years? Why do banks and corporations have billions of dollars of cash value polices all over the country? Why have the wealthy been putting much of their family's wealth for generations into policies? Could it be that they know more about money than you or I do? Could they know more about money than your insurance agent or financial planner? You bet they do! Here are the high points as to why many people who are shown the power of a properly designed policy want to put large amounts of monies into life insurance contracts. Here is a list of benefits to that kind of policy:

1. Guaranteed principle (money cannot go backwards at the whim of any market)
2. Contractually guaranteed growth of your account
3. Dividends paid to policy holders are not taxable

4. Monies grow tax-free

5. Access to monies anytime, at any age, for any reason, without penalty

6. Total control of what you use your money for, be it investment or personal reasons

7. Ability to put in large sums of money to fund your "perpetual financing system," unlike qualified government plans

8. When done properly, all growth and dividends can be taken out, tax-free, for life

9. Ability to use account to recapture lost principle and interest payments

10. Account is judgment- and creditor-proof, both during growth and for withdrawals (depends on the state but is always another layer of protection for your money)

11. Funds pass tax-free to your desired heirs (subject to limits)

12. Easy, cheap, guaranteed access to funds to borrow from regardless of credit, income, or job status. Payments need not be made if you choose (during your working lifetime, you want to make payments to increase your wealth, but they are not mandatory, so if you run into financial hard times, stop payments if you wish with no risk of any collection steps from insurance company)

13. Guaranteed insurability once put in place, regardless of change in physical condition

14. Ability to combine with the world of real estate and private lending to create more tax-free wealth (more on this in another chapter)

15. Death benefit leaves more money behind after you die, tax-free, to your family or whomever you choose

I can promise you that less than 1% of insurance agents know all the benefits of these types of polices that we just discussed. So therefore, they cannot show these benefits to their clients. Most of the time, they don't even attempt to sell these benefits because they themselves believe the hype about term insurance being cheaper than whole life and a better program. Insurance agents take the path of least resistance and put their clients into polices that are not even close to optimal.

These are not your Father's or Mother's insurance policies and it is up to you to be your own judge about what makes sense to you for you and your family's financial future. Why not get a no obligation policy illustration completed and have a 30-minute phone consultation with me or one of my expert team members? Simply go to www.perpetualfinancingsystem.com and request a free phone interview. We can answer all of your questions over the phone and build you a customized policy based on your needs.

Chapter Eight

DO YOUR INVESTMENTS DO ALL OF THIS?

I think we would be mistaken not to compare other places you can put money and hope it grows and provides financial security. Remember, I am not a certified financial planner and never will have that designation. I am just a high school failure and college dropout who has made millions of dollars in revenue and even lost my fair share of money. I have been successful in several different businesses including real estate and insurance. I try to explain everything from that perspective. I believe in keeping things simple. Investing can be a very complicated topic and tens of thousands of books have been written on the topic. We won't even scratch the surface of all that you can do with your money. That is not the purpose of this book or training program. We will just ask you to take out a piece of paper and write down all the places you have your money. There is a difference between types of investments and different accounts those investments can be held in. Most people think their 401(k) is an investment or their IRA is an investment vehicle. That simply is not true. Those accounts are "types" of accounts that are referred to as qualified plans. What or who qualifies them, you ask? Your old Uncle Sam qualifies those accounts and puts many types of rules and regulations as to what you can and can't do with the money once it is put inside those types of accounts. Those types of accounts are tax advantaged in one way or another (or are they?). You take a tax deduction off of your current year income tax when you contribute money into some of these accounts. Any growth inside of those accounts (and growth is by no means guaranteed) is tax deferred until your retirement or a certain age, when it will then be taxed. Roth IRAs do not allow you to take a tax deduction for the money put inside of these accounts, but in return any potential growth will never be taxable. (based on today's rules) These are all qualified plans that the government has come up with to give Americans a way to have a tax-advantaged way to grow money for retirement. I would submit to you that these plans really favor your old Uncle Sam and not you and your family.

Some people refer to these programs as scams for suckers and curse the government for setting up complicated scams designed to enrich your Uncle Sam and not you or me. Uncle Sam qualifies the plans and makes all the rules like how much you can put in, what you can do with it, what is taxable and what isn't, when you have to take it out, how it is taxed, and many other scenarios. So I would simply submit to you that if Uncle Sam qualifies the plans, he is in total control and can change the rules anytime he sees fit. If you don't think that can happen, you don't have to look any further than our beloved social security system, which is the biggest qualified plan in history. This, I believe, has been the biggest theft of wealth in history. It was sold to the public as our friendly Uncle Sam taking a little bit out of our income and putting away in trust for us so we could have a retirement income. It was also supposed to help people who are not capable of working or who are disabled to provide funds that those people do not end up on the street with no resources. What it has morphed into is the single biggest robbery of all time. The funds have been included in operating budgets for generations and the "trust money" is long since gone and replaced with IOUs from our friendly old Uncle Sam. In other words, cash is gone but we will pay you later. Oh and by the way, along the road of this massive robbery, Uncle Sam has changed the rules many times. Mostly how much you pay in (always more) and when you can start to withdraw your money out (always later). So in effect, the government has stolen all the money and now is telling us, who put the money in that we can only take it out when they tell us we can. There should be massive surpluses in that fund and instead, as of this writing, the federal government is projecting a shortfall of 45 billion dollars this year (2012) and more to follow, unless something is done.

Here is another theft from you and me: the government also says that if you want to collect this money (your money, by the way) that you can only make so much money before they start deducting your "benefit." I love that they call it a benefit instead of what it is: them giving me my own money back. If I have put my money in, why should I be penalized for making more money and be threatened with not getting my own money out? They basically say that you can make $14,000 a year without affecting your social security check. For every two dollars you make after that, your social security check gets reduced by a dollar? Steal my money, change all the rules, and then penalize me for being productive and making too much money? As if $14,000 is a lot of income? This is a pure hijacking in every sense of the word. Why don't they just tell us we spent the money, you are not getting it back and too bad, so sad? Instead they are going to make us put more money in and then raise the collection age to 101 years of age before you can start to draw on it!

So why would you think that your 401(k)s and IRAs are safe from such abuse? The truth is the government would love to seize every private qualified plan in the country and then social securitize those same accounts. It is estimated that there are 10 trillion dollars in private qualified plans as of this writing and Uncle Sam is drooling at getting his hands on it in some form or fashion. It might look something like this: Mr. Jones has $250,000 in one of the qualified accounts above and Uncle Sam decides that he will take that money and annuitize the money. In other words, Mr. Jones will get $1,500 per month (or any figure the government deems) until his death, at which time the money will stop and that $250,000 is now gone and property of Uncle Sam. There have even been actual rumblings of this from the most left wing section of the government. The fact that this theft can even be suggested over a cup of coffee in Congress lets me know that there is no limit to Uncle Sam's grasp. He is making all the rules in these qualified plans and can change the rules any time he sees fit. I hope what I have suggested never comes to pass and if it is ever attempted, the architects of this plan are brought up on larceny charges and any other legal term used to describe robbery.

When I suggest this is even a possibility to people in my classes, almost every class will have someone who rightly says, "What is to stop Uncle Sam from doing the same to life insurance contracts?" This is a great question and nobody really knows the answer for sure as there are so many variables. I do think there are some points worth making in this discussion.

1. The contract between you and the insurance company is a private agreement and currently not subject to the same government regulations as your qualified plans. These are not qualified plans and operate under a framework of laws

that have been in existence since before the Internal Revenue Service was a government agency.

2. If the government should decide to go after these contracts and change the rules, they certainly can try and may do so someday. It will require debate, discussion, and a boatload of lawsuits. I would think that life insurance companies and policyholders will not let that happen without a huge fight. Who do you think has a more powerful lobby in congress than insurance companies? My bet would be nobody because nobody has as much money as the insurance companies. With that kind of wealth comes clout and power. Insurance companies have trillions of dollars under management and truth be told, combined as a group, have more money than the government does to spend on lobby and lawsuits. This is one of the only times that a private industry can bring just as much, if not more, power to bear in the legal fight. So first, the idea of robbing insurance companies would have to get past the powerful lobby and then the government has to be ready for a legal fight that could take decades. I like my chances with the insurance companies on my side for a change.

3. Now let's assume for the sake of example that Uncle Sam is successful in changing the tax advantages of your life insurance policy. Does that make your policy not attractive to you as a place to park money (capitalize your private pool of funds) and have it grow? Let's say they gave it the same tax treatment as a 401(k) where the growth was tax-deferred and then you were taxed on the profit when you took it out. Look at the following page where I describe all the benefits of a properly designed life insurance policy. Now simply take out the point about tax free withdrawals. Now look at all the other benefits and ask

yourself if you have anything else that touches it. The answer will still be NOT EVEN CLOSE!

4. One last point about Uncle Sam budding in to life insurance contracts. How many senators and congressman have these kinds of accounts? Remember how much money banks and major corporations have inside these policies as well. Between these last two factors, I believe it would be difficult for Uncle Sam to raid these accounts in comparison to just changing the qualified plan rules.

Now let's talk about some common things people do with their investment dollars and how they compare. I was going to break them all down but then I thought that has been done to death in many other books and there is no need here. I will only refer back to all the benefits above and ask you to take your best shot to beat all those benefits or even come close. So take the best investment you have ever had and put it in a tax advantaged qualified plan and then ask yourself how many of the 15 high points your investments hit:

1. Guaranteed principle (money cannot go backwards at the whim of any market)
2. Contractually guaranteed growth of your account
3. Dividends paid to policy holders are not taxable
4. Monies grow tax-free
5. Access to monies anytime, at any age, for any reason, without penalty
6. Total control of what you use your money for, be it investment or personal reasons
7. Ability to put in large sums of money to fund your "perpetual financing system," unlike qualified government plans

8. When done properly, all growth and dividends can be taken out, tax-free, for life

9. Ability to use account to recapture lost principle and interest payments

10. Account is judgment- and creditor-proof, both during growth and for withdrawals(check state rules)

11. Funds pass tax-free to your desired heirs(check amount maximum)

12. Easy, cheap, guaranteed access to funds to borrow from regardless of credit, income, or job status. Payments need not be made if you choose (during your working lifetime, you want to make payments to increase your wealth, but they are not mandatory, so if you run into financial hard times, stop payments if you wish with no risk of any collection steps from insurance company)

13. Guaranteed insurability once put in place, regardless of change in physical condition

14. Ability to combine with the world of real estate and private lending to create more tax-free wealth (more on this in another chapter)

15. Death benefit leaves more money behind after you die, tax-free, to your family or whomever you choose

I have asked this question in many dozens of classes and asked which one of your...

1. Stocks
2. Bonds
3. Mutual Funds
4. Real Estate
5. Certificate of Deposits

6. Savings accounts
7. Options
8. Oil well leases
9. Notes
10. Tax Liens

... and four hundred other investments offer all of these benefits? You have my contact information and if you have anything that offers all of those points (or even 10 of those benefits) send me an email and let me know. Not one person has sent me an email yet that could say they met that criteria. I don't need to go through all the extra effort to break down every investment you could make. When you look at it this way, there is no doubt that you should take a serious look at reallocating some of your assets into this vehicle. Here is where I must do the proper thing and tell you to consult with your financial advisor. (GOOD LUCK WITH THAT! J) Do you think their response will be good when you tell them you are taking $100,000 out of their accounts and opening up one of these polices? Number one, please don't think they will understand the policy or the volume and velocity you want to do through that policy. The problem with learning these things is that you are almost in a league by yourself. Number two is they have zero financial gain and nothing but a financial loss if you reallocate some funds from your account with them to one of these polices. They are supposed to look above and beyond that and do what is in your best interest but everyone is human and nobody likes to have their income cut. Your best bet is to give them a copy of this book and hope they will give it a look. But I did my job and said CONSULT WITH YOUR FINANCIAL ADVISOR AND THAT I AM NOT A CERTIFIED FINANCIAL PLANNER.

Here is also another point that was driven home for me by a man who has been getting people into these polices for years. He is licensed to sell any financial product he wishes but chooses to exclusively offer clients properly designed life insurance policies. He asked a room full of financial professionals very soon after a dramatic drop in the stock market how many of them can honestly say that not one client lost a dime in the most recent stock market collapse. There were about 200 financial professionals in the room and they all laughed under their breath but not one raised their hand. He waited about 30 seconds for the laughter to quit and he slowly raised his hand. You see when you put money into this type of vehicle; you insulate your funds from drops in the market. You don't lose 40% of your account value in a few days or weeks. Remember, your principle is contractually guaranteed and so is your growth. You can magnify that growth by using your capitalized money inside of your life insurance contract and take loans out against the policy (and eventually use that money and loan funds to others after you have been trained properly on how to do that as safely as possible) and pay that money back with at least the same interest and payments you would have paid a finance company. Not one of those financial professionals could honestly raise their hands. Which one of them could have been your certified financial planner?

With all that being said, if you have an investment or two you like to use to help you make money, than by all means continue to use that investment vehicle. You may just want to treat your family finance like a business or successful financing pool and think of allocating 20 to 40% of your available funds to setting up a properly designed whole life insurance contract. I would suggest this to you as a way to make more money on your investments. Borrow the money for whatever investment you want to make from your insurance policy first, and then make the investment. What a simple, powerful concept! Borrow your funds from your own financing pool and do your stock, real estate, private loan, tax lien, etc. deal and set up a payment plan to pay back pool of funds to your insurance policy.

You need to start thinking of your policy as a true financing pool that you own and control. You must manage it that way as well. Everyone who borrows money pays it back with interest no matter what and no matter who borrows them money. That especially goes for you and any family member. This will not only assure that your insurance policy is always growing tax-free but in many cases it may have a positive income tax situation on whatever investment you make. Here is a very basic example.

(Short term and long term taxes are always in flux and this example is not meant to show actual numbers but only as an example to illustrate a point. Please check with your own tax specialist)

$50,000	of your non-qualified plan money to buy a stock you think is a winner
$10,000	profit from the sale of the stock in one year
$10,000	taxable at 30% means you net $7,000

This time we do the following:

$50,000	loan from your insurance policy, (in actuality we are borrowing the monies from the life insurance company's general fund and using our cash to collateralize that loan) payable at 10% back to policy
$5,000	profit goes back to the policy at the end of the year, no tax due
$10,000	gross profit on stock deal
-$5,000	interest for loan to do the deal
$5,000	gross profit
30%	tax rate means you keep $3,500 plus the $5,000 tax-free profit to your financing pool. Now you net $8,500 instead of $7,000! That is over a 20% difference

This difference gets much bigger with real estate investments and we will discuss that in another upcoming chapter.

So in summary, do your investment deal but pay your financing pool back no matter if you make money or lose money. If you make money, you will pay less tax. If you lose money, your pool of funds will still be profitable, thus lowering your loss on the investment. Be true to your financing pool and it will be true to you. You now have your core business or job, whatever they may be; and you have your financing pool that is cranking out tax-free profits for the rest of your life, creating generational wealth. Why didn't I learn this system 20 years before? Why didn't you? We don't really know but we know it now and it is our responsibility to get it set up and operating as soon as possible for our family and ourselves.

Chapter Nine

USE YOUR OWN FINANCING POOL TO SET UP A REAL ESTATE CASH FLOW MACHINE

Wealth Tip: Buying cash flow properties can be a great asset for the right investor. If you would like to find out more about creating a passive real estate income machine please visit our site for a free audio download which will help you get started. Just go to: <u>www.perpetualfinancingsystem. com/realestatecashflow</u> for your free download.

This chapter is near and dear to my heart because I get to share with you a very powerful program that you can easily combine with your new financing policy to create additional wealth and income. I know real estate investment has been much maligned lately in the press due to all the negative news about real estate and the huge foreclosure boom. Maybe even you yourself have seen your own holdings or your own home dramatically lose value over the last few years. I am sure many people reading this have even gone through a foreclosure on either your own personal home or an investment home. I went through my own personal blood bath when the subprime mortgage market blew up and the real estate markets tanked at the same time.

So if that's the case, then why in the world am I suggesting to you that you consider combining the Perpetual Finance System with real estate? The answer is easy but the explanation will take a little time. The simple answer is because the real estate debacle has created more opportunity than ever before in our country to build wealth. Warren Buffet (a man who knows a thing or two about money) has been credited with this quote: "When others are greedy be fearful but when others are fearful be greedy." This quote could not describe any more accurately how I feel about today's real estate market. In many areas of the country, prices are down 50% and more from their highs of just a few years ago. If it is not like that where you live... move! No, I am not actually suggesting you move just to invest in real estate because with technology today there is no need for that. You may be sitting with enough inventory right in your own backyard to retire in just a few short years.

A thousand books and seminars have been presented on real estate investment and I have read and attended more than my share. I have also had the good fortune to train thousands of real estate investors all over North America on how to make money in the real estate business. I have made a fortune in real estate, lost a fortune in real estate, and am now in the process of making a bigger fortune in real estate than I had the last time. I would submit to you that you should be building your own fortune during the biggest buyers market in American history. However, there are too many ways to count on how to make money in real estate and with literally dozens and dozens of strategies at your disposal. Don't panic as we will not be discussing even a few of them. We will be focusing on one main strategy to build a cash flow machine. The strategy will not be applicable in all areas but is certainly applicable to all people who have an interest and a little bit of capital. That strategy is simply buying distressed properties that need a little cosmetic work, repairing them, and leasing them out to good tenants for cash flow. Now if you live in high dollar areas like the west coast or east coast areas, this strategy will not apply to you, but no need to worry as I have dozens of students in high dollar areas that I am helping implement this strategy from the comfort of their own living room no matter where they live. I will give a group of you the opportunity to do the same things they are doing, if you wish.

We must first discuss the reason we will be spending the bulk of your time on this strategy. There are a few simple reasons to focus on this strategy:

1. Abundance of quality deals in the right market places
2. Simple to implement
3. Huge cash on cash returns
4. Very little money needed to get started
5. No need for risky bank mortgages
6. Strategy is not dependant on home values going up
7. Ability to retire with a six figure passive income in 5-8 years
8. Tax-free income to live in and have a great lifestyle

Let's discuss them in more in depth.

Number one: Abundance of quality deals in the right market places

The last few years have seen the largest numbers of foreclosures in history in many areas of the country. Some locations (like mine, for instance) have not seen prices this low since the 1960s! You can go out in those marketplaces today, if you have some training and some trusted "boots on the ground" and buy properties for huge discounts off of their highs. In some cities you can buy great homes in great areas for dirt-cheap prices and rent them out for great positive cash flows. Some cities are better than others for this strategy and it will depend not only on prices but also on local rental markets and rental values. I am going to talk about one area in particular that I believe is the best place in the United States to buy high quality homes in lovely areas for deep discounts. What makes this particular location so attractive from the investment and cash flow standpoint is that you have the ability to buy homes at 1950 and 1960 prices but with 2012 rental values.

I have visited every major city in North America and in many of them I have had the opportunity to look at real estate and see what those markets had to offer. From a pure cash flow and cash-on-cash return perspective, I can tell you that this particular market has not been equaled by any other place I have visited. This particular city has been hit very hard by the recent depression (at least in this city it was a full-blown depression in economic terms) and its local residents have endured some very tough times. Let's not keep you in suspense any longer; this city is also the vacation capital of North America. You should be guessing this location easily now. When I discuss this live, people shout that this city is Orlando, Las Vegas, Phoenix, Miami, New York, Washington D.C., and other big, beautiful cities that they think are the vacation capital of North America. I tell them the vacation capital has been and will always be… Detroit Michigan!

Now after the laughter has died down, I ask them what they are laughing at and if anyone has ever vacationed in Detroit. There is almost always one brave soul that raises their hands amid the laughter of the crowd. Okay, so maybe Detroit is not the vacation capital of the North America but I share with them what it is the capital of and that is "real estate cash flow champion." Now that you know that, what are you waiting for to get going on your cash flow machine? Just fly to Detroit and start buying! But wait, it might take a little more information before you could or should consider starting your own real estate cash flow machine. You will need to be convinced that Metro Detroit is really a secret gold mine of cash flow properties. I know this to be true because I have talked to more than a couple people on this topic. (deleted a fragmented sentence) I cannot convince anyone who is totally not coachable, but if you are open-minded and coachable, listen to why Metro Detroit is a gold mine for real estate investors and why people are coming from all over the world to buy in that marketplace.

First of all let me tell you I am a lifelong resident of Metro Detroit. My dad was a Detroit Police Officer for just under 30 years and we lived in the city of Detroit proper. However, I do not invest in, nor do any of our clients that listen to our training, actually buy properties in the city of Detroit. We invest in the suburbs of Detroit. You see folks, you can buy nice quality homes in desirable suburban locations for $20,000 to $50,000 and lease these homes out for $800 to $1,200 per month depending on actual location and amenities of the particular home. These houses are in nice areas with good schools, parks, roads, etc. They are places you can feel safe at anytime of the day or night. Now, before I have my fellow Detroiters telling me what a louse I am for not sending people to the city to invest, we need to get a couple things straight. I love the city of Detroit and lived there for my first 20 years of life. That being said we have to be honest that the city has been abused and stolen from through poor management at many levels for decades now. This will not be a political platform book but all one has to do to see the success of previous administrations and city councils is to look at the most recent census statistics. One time, the city of Detroit boasted over 2 million people in its city limits and was considered a sister city (although baby sister) to the city of Chicago. The 2010 census shows a population of a little over 700,000, which is obviously a huge reversal of fortune. Populations do not shift that much unless a city is really screwing things up in a big way. That tells you that people are not happy with their circumstances in the city and are choosing to live elsewhere. Most people outside of the Metro Detroit area think that the population decrease means that Detroit is a ghost town and expect to see tumbleweeds going down the streets. While it is true the city has experienced a huge population decrease, the areas around the city (suburbs) have seen their populations explode over that same time frame. So it is not that all the people left the area, they just left the city proper for the suburbs. In fact, the Metro Detroit area actually has over 4 million people who live there so don't believe all the hype on CNN. There are several economic reasons I do not tell anyone, including my clients, to buy properties in the city itself at this time and for the foreseeable future:

1. Property taxes are higher than almost anyplace else in the Metro area, negatively affecting your cash flow (be sure to find out what your non-homestead taxes are going to be as opposed to what they might be now, as they will be going up)
2. Insurance is higher in the city as well, further taking away from that cash flow
3. The school district has a 70% drop out rate
4. Low quality city services (city workers are good workers but they are always asked to do more with less, affecting the quality of the service)
5. Lower rents than in adjoining counties

These are the main reasons I do not recommend anyone invest in the city of Detroit proper. I will finish this point with a true story.

One night a few years ago, I received a call from a business associate who lives in Montreal. He had a client who just informed him he had purchased a property in Detroit. His client had only called him after all the money had changed hands. After a discussion my friend was able to obtain some details of the deal. The home was in the city of Detroit. The purchase price was $17,000 and he was told he could rent the home for $700.00 for a great cash flow. He did almost no other research and closed on the deal. My friend thought something might be wrong so he called me for my opinion as the local expert. He just had to tell me the cross streets and I knew his client had been robbed. The home was in a total warzone and was worth nowhere near $17,000. In fact, after a little research I found out the company who sold it to him was out of Florida and had bought the home the previous month for $2,000 and did nothing to it and sold it to this man for $17,000 using an online auction sale. The investor who bought the home was from Vancouver, where the average sale price of a home is $1,000,000, so when you see a brick home for $17,000 you almost figure that you can't lose. Well you can't lose that much but you can lose your $17,000 very easily if you don't know what you're doing and don't have boots on the ground you can trust.

I agreed to talk to the investor from Vancouver who bought the property to confirm to him what I had found. He became upset, but not with himself. He seemed to get upset with me for being the bearer of bad news. I informed him that he must not have done any homework and he was going to lose his investment. He became upset but he really had nobody to be upset at except for himself. He violated the rules of investing in real estate and one of those basic rules is performing due diligence. The information I shared with him was available to him if he had only spent 15 minutes verifying some details before he invested.

That gentleman from Vancouver could have made a great investment just a few miles down the road if he would have had me and my team working with him, but he chose to go it on his own and blew $17,000 of his hard-earned money. We could have gotten him a quality home in a quality area for maybe just a few thousand dollars more. The home would have been in a safe area and would have rented for $800.00 per month, minimum, for a great cash flow coming from his investment. He had no idea his taxes were going to go up dramatically and what his insurance would be after he closed. This will never happen to one of our clients, because we work with them step-by-step to get them quality investments with cash flow for years to come.

The bottom line is this: when it comes to investing in homes in Detroit proper, DON'T DO IT! Not until the city gets serious about its future and elects quality people that attract quality businesses back to the city limits. Until then, there is a fortune to be had in the suburbs. My team can help you put this plan into action. Feel free to visit us online and take a free recorded webinar on investing in Metro Detroit at www.recashflowmachine.com. You can also watch videos of real life deals we have acquired for our clients. If you would like to discuss becoming a client of ours, feel free to get in touch with us to book your trip to Metro Detroit.

There are other places in the country that have inexpensive properties where this basic concept will work well. Much of the southeast and southwest has similar deals but none are as good as what we have available in Metro Detroit. Find an area you like and implement this money machine right away. Those prices will not always be this low so jump on this opportunity and run hard and fast!

Number two: Simple to implement

Real estate investment is filled with complicated and creative strategies to acquire properties. While there are many valid ways to put together creative deals, this is the simplest, most straightforward way to build a cash flow machine, starting with your own assets. You will then use that cash flow to acquire more assets. Using this rapid method of building wealth you will be able to retire with a six figure passive income stream in 5 to 10 years depending on how much you are willing to start with and how fast you are willing to implement this program. I will show you my 8-7-6 program soon. Six figure income in eight years and a seven figure net worth. This is a powerful program we will go over in depth in another chapter.

Number three: Huge cash on cash returns

First of all, let's talk about what is a simple cash-on-cash return. It works like this: take the amount of your money you have in an investment and divide that number by the net income you receive from that investment. So for simple math: Let's look at an investment where you have $30,000 cash invested. We will assume that the money bought you a single-family home that will rent for $800.00 per month. Now the bad news is you don't get to keep all of the $800.00 every month. We will assume you have $300.00 per month in management fees, property taxes, insurance and deferred maintenance and a small vacancy factor. That will leave you with a $500.00 net income and then you multiply that monthly figure x 12 months to get an annual net income of $6,000. So you take your net income of $6,000 and divide that number by your investment of $30,000 to get your annual cash on cash return of 20%.

If you can consistently get 20% cash-on-cash return on your investments you are going to grow your money exponentially. There is an old rule of money called the rule of 72 and it says that if you want to find out how long it will take to double your money, you just take your rate of return (cash-on-cash) and divide it into 72 and that figure will tell you how long it takes for your money to double. So if you take your cash-on-cash return of 20% and divide that into 72, you get 3.6 years to double your $30,000 investment assuming no taxes. That is very possible using the system outlined in this book. Even if you only were able to generate a 12 to 14% cash on cash return your wealth will grow nicely.

Now let me be very honest. In the example above, it is possible that you may not get your rent from some tenants and have to evict them and re-rent the home. You may even have to clean it up and put some more money into the home. That is not the norm, however, it will happen from time to time. So it is possible that the 20% cash-on-cash return may be less in some years depending on what you have to do with the unit. Some years there will be no expenses or vacancy and you will get your 20%, cash-on-cash. Other years you will have more expenses and that number may go down to 8 to 12%, this is still strong cash-on-cash return.

Number four: Very little money to get started

Never before has it been so easy to get started being a real estate investor with such little money, while at the same time getting such a high rent-to-value ratio. If you can get your hands on $25,000 to $50,000, you can acquire a solid home in a nice area that could provide a great income and return on your money. You then can take the rents and pour them back into your financing pool inside of your insurance policy, which will enable you to put the principles of volume and velocity to work for you with very little money to start your program. So, that money goes into your policy and it qualifies for growth and dividends, which will build more wealth for you other than just the rental income. This is true compound interest working for you on a tax-advantaged basis. Now, when you are able to get $25,000 to $50,000 back into that policy, you borrow it out again from the insurance company using your funds as collateral and buy a second income-producing asset that will now put $1,000 per month of net income into your financing pool system. Now you are starting to see the program here. This is like a shampoo bottle that says rinse and repeat. You build your holdings up with rental profits and not leverage debt. Your empire is built on a foundation of bedrock instead of a house of cards financed by personally guaranteed debt. You are taking profits and using them to acquire more cash producing assets, and you are continuing to increase your holdings, net worth, and passive income.

Doing real estate with this model and the ability to volumize and velocitize monies in this way was not possible until the real estate collapse of a few years ago, that continues today in most areas of the country. You have the unique opportunity to buy prices in a time warp. Buying at 1960s prices and leasing at 21st century prices! This is the opportunity of a lifetime and you should get a piece of the great American fire sale for you and your family. Ask yourself this question. If it was 2003 and a home was retailing for $120,000 to homeowners, and someone came to you and said you could buy that home for $30,000, would you have done that deal? The answer in 2003 would have been an overwhelming yes from almost everyone reading this book. You would have laughed and said, "if only you could do that." Well, now you can do that, so I don't know why more people don't look at it that way and start buying with both fists. If you don't, you will be sitting a few years in the future when these same homes could be selling for $60,000 to $80,000 and you could have tripled your money, plus all the positive cash flow, saying, "I should have jumped on those deals." Go out and get 5, 10, or more deals to produce long-term passive income and potential large backend cash when the market turns. Call my team today to make this a reality for you and your family.

Number 5: No need for risky bank mortgages

We are currently going through the biggest foreclosure boom in history and you cannot have a foreclosure without first borrowing money. Every real estate book or course ever written will tell you to use OPM or "other people's money" to leverage your fortune. When I started my first life in real estate I bought into that philosophy 110% and went out and borrowed many millions of dollars in mortgages. I made money on almost every deal and that philosophy seemed to be the right way to do real estate. Now, after making a boatload of money and losing a boatload of money, I have altered my position somewhat on the issue of using borrowed funds to create wealth.

The basic idea is to use someone else's money to acquire the asset, then turn the payments over to someone else during the time you own it, and then sell it years later for much more than you paid. Seems simple but how about when it goes down dramatically instead of going up? Now you are what is known as "upside-down" on the property and at risk of foreclosure, credit problems, and lawsuits by creditors. If it goes hard against you, it is very possible to get wiped out and lose all that you have and more. How could you lose more? Many times, and depending on the state you are doing business in, it is possible for lenders to file suit on you personally for any loss they might suffer for the loan they granted you for your deal. So how about spending all your money to keep those deals afloat and then, after you have expended all your cash and still were not able to keep your leverage house of cards standing, your creditors can come after you for the "deficiency" on your loan. That does not apply in every state, but it does apply to many and you need to know this before you decide to build wealth with borrowed money.

When prices are high, there is almost no choice for people but to borrow money to acquire real estate. When prices are low, it is not necessary for most people to have to borrow money in the form of a mortgage or deed of trust from a local bank or other financing source. This means that your cash flow machine is built on equity and cash flow and not on leveraging debt. You may build starting with a very modest sum of money and leverage the income from that to acquire more cash-producing assets. What I just described to you is the very term "compound interest" or "profits-on-profits." It is so easy to talk about, but so difficult to actually achieve in the real world. You have it with this simple plan if you will just have enough for sight and guts to make it a reality. Not only will your cash flow and equity grow systematically with these wise real estate investments but by setting up your insurance policy FIRST, then using that as your own personal and business financing pool, and have it loan out money to do your real estate deals, then you are achieving the elusive "triple dip" and creating wealth rapidly.

I will be showing you how to take $100,000 and, by implementing the strategies in this book, turn it into over $120,000 a year in income. At the same time, you could have (if the market just turns around a little) a 7 figure net worth with about 20 paid-for homes. On top of that, you will also have the original $100,000 back into the policy plus about $60,000 in extra tax-free cash. This can all be done in about 7 to 8 years of starting to implement the plan. I call it my 876 plan, which stands for 6 figure income + seven figure net worth + 8 years. You can also get a recorded presentation of me showing a group of investors this program. Some of them are already working with me to make this a reality in their own lives and have properties producing income for them right now. The only difference between them and you is timing. They were exposed a little bit sooner than you so they are farther down their road than you are yours.

Number 6: Not dependent on prices going up

So many books and real estate programs are all dependent on prices going up from their current position. In other words, SPECULATION! If you had been practicing those types of strategies in the last 5 years, you would have almost certainly gone bankrupt. By using my system, if values go up in the next few years it will be gravy for the participants. You will be implementing this program and really not even caring if prices rebound. I personally believe that in the next few years, prices will start to rebound in many areas of the country. Here are some signs to look for:

a. Current foreclosure levels will start to decrease, stemming from the glut of properties on the market. This is a must for prices to rebound at all

b. Banks start to loosen their purse strings and start to lend out money more easily. This will fuel growth and prices because there is already the pent-up demand for housing

c. Consumer confidence starts to rebound and unemployment rates drop, giving people the power to buy again

d. It will take many people two to three years to put their foreclosures or bankruptcies behind them, allowing their credit scores to rebound and making them buyers again

I believe all of those events are 24 to 36 months off, but certainly have no crystal ball. I would not recommend that any strategy you use rely on values coming back anytime soon. I would also not advise you to leverage your holdings with personally guaranteed bank mortgages. The strategies in this program will help you acquire assets at rock bottom prices that produce fantastic cash flow. When you implement this strategy, you can achieve forced growth without the rebounding of prices. The truth of the matter from a pure investment strategy standpoint is most people will not be in a big hurry for prices to rebound. If you are buying great homes in nice areas for $25,000 to $50,000 and leasing them for between $800 and $1,200 per month, you will not be in a hurry for that gold mine to dry up. When prices do rebound, it will mean that your current holdings are worth more, but it will be harder to buy deals in those price ranges. So the moral of the story is start to build this today and not tomorrow. Now using the program I am about to go over, you will end up with about 20 homes in just a few short years. These homes will be free and clear or the loans will be by your own self controlled pool of funds through your properly designed life insurance policy. This will give you the money to pay back the loans or let the loans ride and put your money toward cash value and growth. I will give you a couple examples using an actual life insurance policy illustration.

Take the time to study those illustrations so you can begin to see the power of this system. You will see some really big numbers start to take shape in your family's financial future. They are not too good to be true. On the contrary, they are real life numbers that are very doable if you will work this simple plan. If values do bounce back over the next several years, you will be all the better off, but this plan really does not rely on values going up. I know many homeowners in the Metro Detroit area will hate me for saying this, but I hope values do not start to bounce upward for 5 to 7 years because that will allow myself and my clients to acquire many more cash producing assets that that will add to our passive incomes and net worth. Those homes will also allow huge tax-free growth inside of our policies. Now that we have discussed the possibility of implementing my 876 plan, let's take a look at some real numbers and some breakdowns of numbers. Get ready for a bumpy and exciting ride!

Number 7: Producing a 6 figure passive income and 7 figure net worth in 5 to 8 years

This is my favorite part of this book and training system to show people because it is so simple and yet so powerful. Better than those two it is actually DOABLE!! This is not theory, but real life numbers and doable deals. I know, because we are setting these programs up every week for not only ourselves, but our clients as well. If you qualify for the program and to work with me and my team, we can also help you make this a reality.

Let's start by capitalizing your financing pool through your properly designed whole life insurance policy. Put enough money into the policy to be able to borrow out $100,000 of cash value. That means you might have to put in about $120,000 to start the policy. You will give up access to the additional $20,000 for a short period of time only. Within a few short years, you will have more in the policy than you put in and it only grows and gets better and more efficient as time goes by, and more growth and dividends grow inside that policy. So we assume we can borrow out $100,000 in this example. If you don't have that much money to start that does not mean you can't begin this program. You can absolutely start this program if you have a mere $25,000 to invest. The numbers will just grow a little slower and it will require some more time to achieve the same results. The program will still work very well with less money. The other side of the coin is also true so if you have more funds to start, you can achieve more income, more assets, and in less time than with this example. The main point is that you start with what you can, but make sure you start. My team and I can help you make this a reality from wherever you are starting from but it will be up to you to start.

If you are wondering how to start this program and who can help you, please look no further than my email address and website. Contact my team today and we will not only get your policy funded, but we can also walk you step-by-step and help you acquire cash-producing assets. Just get in contact with my team today at www.perpetualfinancingsystem.com and tell us you would like to see your real life numbers and are ready to put this program to work. We are in a unique position not only to train you but also to set up the whole program for you and work with you to implement it immediately.

We now have our policy funded and have access to $100,000 and we borrow it out over the next couple months to acquire 4 single-family homes for an average of $25,000 each. We then lease these properties out for you for an average of $800.00 per month at the low end. So that is $3,200 in income from those buildings. You do not get to keep all that money of course as there will be expenses associated with the owning and operating of these homes. You will have to pay property taxes, insurance, management, and deferred maintenance. We will assume all of that will cost you $300.00 per month, which will leave us $500.00 per month or $6,000 of net operating income per year. If you invested $25,000 that would be a 24% cash-on-cash return. So using the rule of 72 you are on pace to double your investment in about 3 years. That is how to grow wealth exponentially! However, let's be both fair and realistic about that rate of return. When you own real estate there are always additional and unforeseen expenses such as leaky faucets, hot water tanks, air conditioning compressors, losses from evictions, etc. So please don't think every year will be those kinds of cash-on-cash returns. Expect the unexpected and you will be prepared. With that being said, you also want to realize I also did not put in any rental increases and I used the low end of the rent spectrum. So if you lease for a little higher that will offset some of the other expenses we discussed. I truly believe these numbers are very accurate but if they turn out to be only 70% as good as we discuss, they are still fantastic!

Now we are going to use the net operating income from all 4 units and put them back into our financing pools (insurance policies.) Our policies will take in $24,000 from our cash producing houses. Let's also flow through an additional $10,000 of our money (fresh money from our income or other assets) back through the policy. So now we have $34,000 back into our policies at the beginning of year two. We now velocitize our money just like a bank would by loaning it back out and we acquire one more solid cash flow piece of real estate. Now our net income is $2,500 or $30,000 from all 5 properties. We are going to flow through the $30,000 back into our policy plus the $10,000 of fresh money. Remember, we also have $9,000 left in our account from last year after we bought our fifth house. So we will have $49,000 of cash value plus let's not forget the growth the insurance company is giving us on that account with guarantees and dividends. That will put us easily over $50,000 of cash value. Now it is time to velocitize again and borrow that money out and buy two more cash flow machines or single-family houses. So now we have 7 homes producing $3,500 per month or $42,000 per year of income plus the $10,000 of fresh money into the policy. We have well over $50,000 of cash value in the account and the ability to buy two more properties. Now we have 9 homes that are spitting out $4,500 per month or $54,000 back into the policy, plus our $10,000 of fresh money, making $64,000 in cash value. Now it is time to repeat the process and buy two more homes, borrowing out $50,000 so now we own 11 homes at $5,500 per month net operating income or $66,000 per year. We also add our $10,000 of fresh money into the policy (plus the $14,000 left in the policy from last year) leaving $90,000 inside our policies. We now borrow out $75,000 and buy 3 new properties, making our net income $7,000 per month or $84,000 by the end of the year, plus our $10,000 of fresh money. With the growth inside of the policy from the insurance company, you will have well over $100,000 of cash value, so now we are going to buy 4 more income producing homes, putting our monthly income to $9,000 per month or $108,000 per year. That money goes back inside our policy, plus the $10,000 of fresh money, giving us over $130,000 of cash value. Now we will repeat this process one last time, acquiring 5 more income properties, putting our income at $11,500 per month or $138,000 of net income.

So now we are 8 years through this program and here is how it looks. We started with just $100,000 but we now have $138,000 of net income from our 23 investment homes. The homes are free and clear from any bank loans. True, there are policy loans, but as you will see in the policy illustrations we have the flexibility to either pay them off with our income from the houses or to let the loans ride and continue putting our income back into the policy toward paid-up additions. To see an actual illustration that just lets the money ride inside the policy for 7 more years (15 years total), and to see that you have become a tax-free cash rich multimillionaire, just contact us so we can show you the numbers above in an actual illustration. What a retirement you have set yourself up for and in a fraction of the time otherwise possible. You have set yourself up to be able to retire on a quarter million dollars a year income and most of that will not be taxable. That is the income from your houses and the monies we are going to start accessing through our policies to give us total control of our lives and what we do with our time.

This money machine plan is so powerful that I think everyone who reads this should get it started right away. Unfortunately, I know just a small percentage of people who read this will ever take actual action. That is the difference between high-income millionaires and low-income people who bitch and moan about how they can't get ahead and how everyone is conspiring against them to keep them broke, or at least constantly struggling. Even if the numbers are only 50 to 70% as good as this, ask yourself if you have any other plan at your fingertips that can achieve these results. Then once the answer is not even close, call our team today and tell them you want to have your own real estate and financing money machine. We are the only ones in the country who specializes in this and have access to tens of thousands of properties in our backyard that will fit this plan to a tee.

What will happen for most of you is you will talk yourself out of this and go looking for the next get rich quick plan that is exciting but not doable for most people. The next group will decide this is for you but then make the mistake of getting the opinion of friends of family members about this whole program. I need to make a suggestion about getting business or investment advice from friends and family members. DON'T DO IT!! The fact is the vast majority of your friends and family members have no right to give you financial or business advice. That is akin to getting weight loss advice from fat people. As of this writing, I am what would be referred to in politically correct circles as calorically challenged. I would just say that I am overweight and have been for a good portion of my life. I intend on doing something about it and maybe by the time you have read this book I will have lost a significant amount of weight. If I have not achieved that goal, then would I have any business telling you how to lose weight and be in shape? The answer is absolutely NO WAY! Well, most of your friends or families are broke or at least not financially abundant. Do you think they know how to achieve the results we are talking about here? They will have no clue whatsoever but they will proceed to tell you not to get involved with this because it "sounds too good to be true."

The fact is there are many financial and business scams out there and many people spend endless hours trying to bilk you out of your money. This is just not one of those "things" or one of those times. I just gave a class in Metro Detroit and had a couple get very excited about this concept and what we were teaching. So much so that they approached my partner and me and asked us if we could show them some more properties before they went back to Florida. This is not a married couple, but they are in a long-term, committed relationship. The man is about 73 and the woman is about 64 years of age and they are a pleasure to deal with. When they left town they were both committed to implementing this program and each were going to fund a policy with about $120,000 to start and then begin using the plan above. Once they returned home, the man's family got wind of what was going on and jumped all over my client and told him not to do this program. They have talked him out of both programs and that is a shame as they are the most solid programs available in the marketplace today. After all, they combine two cornerstones of our country's wealth, life insurance and real estate. Sounds like a powerful program to me and it did to them as well. Now all of a sudden, he has talked himself out of it and that is a shame. His kids don't even realize that they have given their Dad bad advice and cost themselves a fortune in later years. After all, whom do you think he is going to leave all those free and clear houses to upon his passing? To the lady's credit, she is proceeding anyway, and will be glad she did. We are giving her a shot at being retired in a few years (which is her goal) with over $6,000 net income every month. That, combined with her social security and modest pension, will give her an income most retirees can only dream about in their later years. I congratulate her for her guts and I hope she will rub off on her companion. By the way, some people assume that if they are too old or have a physical ailment that they can't qualify for an insurance policy. That may or may not be the case but even if you can't qualify due to one of the reasons above, we can take the policy out on someone else's life. How do you think the banks and corporations take out so much insurance? They put the death benefit on others, but they control all the cash value as the owner of the policy. So my client above was going to put the death benefit on his 35-year-old son, so the insurance would be easily obtained. My client would control all the cash value during his lifetime and the son would have zero say so on how that cash was used. The son is just the insured and not the owner of the policy. So if you are a little older or have some health issues, we can set the policy up on someone else's life.

To be fair, if my Dad came home from a real estate seminar from out of town and laid out this plan and started talking about those kinds of dollars, I would tell him he was nuts and try to talk him out of it. That would be human nature, but you must understand, none of his children have any kind of background in this field at all. They really have no credentials or experience regarding how to create or protect wealth, but they are all too ready to advise their dad. Kind of sounds like getting weight loss advice from me, does it not? Be your own council and ask yourself if all of this makes perfect sense. If the answer is yes, then proceed with your program. If it does not sound right to you, then go down another wealth path. We are combining two of the most powerful wealth creators in human history and it is a rock solid program. I hope we will be working together soon to implement this cash flow machine system.

You now not only have a step-by-step blueprint to produce income and wealth but the means to work with a qualified team to make it a reality. This should get your blood pounding and mind racing. I am excited just writing about it and I have been exposed to it for quite some time now. Please remember this point: wealthy people have systems and blueprints, poor people have excuses and the "BUT SYNDROME." You know what the "BUT SYNDROME" is and how it works:

1. BUT what if something goes wrong?
2. BUT what if you can't get your rents?
3. BUT what if Uncle Sam changes the rules?
4. BUT, BUT, BUT, BUT, ETC.

One of my best mentors told me one time, "You can make money or you can make excuses but it is hard to make both." Now is your time to make money and stop with the excuses. If you don't act now, you will be saying "what if" in just a few short years. Go for this hard and work the system with my team's help.

Number 8: Building a tax-free retirement income stream to have a great lifestyle

Now that you have your financing cash flow machine and your real estate cash flow machine built and firing on all cylinders, it is time for you to reap all the benefits. You now have the option to sit back and take in a boatload of money every month or continue to grow your wealth using the same program. Let's say you have been disciplined and followed the program of taking your money from your 23 homes and letting them go back into the policy for another 7 years. You now have over $3,300,000 in your policy. You also have about $140,000 a year coming in in rental income that now you are going to start to spend on whatever you choose. You can also start to utilize the funds inside the policy for retirement and good times. If you want a Ferrari or other fancy automobile, stroke a check and get one. You now have enough cash and cash flow to live a remarkable lifestyle with no job needed. You can travel several times a year on a first class vacation all over the world. You can spend weekends at your own waterfront home or cottage, drive the automobiles of your dreams, set up foundations, and donate to quality charities. You are truly living your dream and you did it because you saw an opportunity and jumped in with both feet.

Not only do you have the income from the rentals, but you can start to easily withdraw funds from your policy. Let's take $120,000 per year out of your policy. You can borrow (not withdraw) all your cash value if you wish without taxes If we take out that money and close down the policy (which would be idiotic) we would have to pay tax on the growth and lose the death benefit on the policy. So we would never consider doing that but we could very easily take out policy loans from the insurance policy and you never have to pay those loans back. How is this possible? Well, first of all the loans will be paid back but we don't have to worry about it in our lifetimes if we choose. Just for this example, let's say you borrow $500,000 out of the policy to add to your rental income in your later years and live like a king or queen. Then you pass away (last time I checked, nobody gets out alive) leaving behind that $500,000 worth of loans that you have never made a payment on in many years. So not only do you owe the $500,000, you also owe $100,000 in interest for round numbers. So on your death the insurance company is owed $600,000, but you have a $2,600,000 death benefit that gets paid to your family upon your death. The insurance company will pay out your benefit, but hold back the money they are owed. So your family gets $2,000,000 net cash to them income tax-free (depending on some other estate issues so please get advice from your tax attorney). By then, they will also have their own financing pools and policies set up that will be performing for them and their families. Your family will know what to do with the $2,000,000 because you will have trained them on the power of money flow and being self financed instead of using the banks. You will be the one who started generational wealth for years to come. So much good can be done if families are taught to use these polices not only to provide wealth to them, but fund foundations, charities, small business banks, etc.

How many of you wish your parents or grandparents would have been thoroughly educated on this program and implemented it 30 to 50 years ago? Yes, you can't help but have a little regret when you really get this and how it works. I really believe this is the best way to create and maintain wealth for generations. I think it is superior to stocks, real estate, or business. You see, you could make a fortune in any of those areas and be an expert in those fields. However, upon your passing, your family members might not have the same talent in those fields and could squander or lose all that wealth because they don't have your skill set. However, anyone can be taught how to control a financing pool and the power of cash flow. The family member just has to maintain premiums into the policy and be a good steward of their money, control their finances and their wealth is guaranteed generationally. Train your family on how money and money flow works and you have truly taught them how to fish for the next hundred years and more. They will be trained on wealth and how to keep it and distribute it to those less fortunate than themselves. Now we are going to talk the power of cash flow real estate.

Chapter Ten

TRULY THE OPPORTUNITY OF A LIFETIME IN CASH FLOW REAL ESTATE

We have a special bonus for all you high income business owners out there who are paying $50,000 to $50,000,000 in federal income taxes. We at perpetual financing work with a top level attorney who shows successful business owners a very specific strategy how to cut your tax liability by 50 to 80% and use the savings to create wealth. If you are sick every quarter when you pay your old uncle sam, please visit our site at www.Perpetualfinancingsystem. Com/taxreduction for a very special package to be mailed to you and a free consultation will be set to show you how this very specific program works. If you think your cpa or tax attorney knows how this works, you are probably very mistaken and could cost you millions of dollars in wasted taxes.

We first thank you for all your help with our first home. Besides being a great instructor, through which you taught us a lot. You were great at answering our questions about this whole process.... We followed your advice and got a toll free number and put the house on our website (that was so easy). We had our first open house on a Sunday. We had an offer four days later and closed on the property in two weeks. Our profit was $25,000.

—Jacqui and Chris Heeder

The real estate market in most parts of the country has been in freefall for the last 3 to 4 years. The foreclosure rate is at its highest ever in recorded history. Many people's equities have been wiped out by this current recession or depression and values will not recover to their former levels for probably decades. That is all terrible news! Or is it? From strictly a consumer's standpoint, it is all terrible news. However, from a businessperson's viewpoint and current real estate investor's viewpoint, it is one of the greatest opportunities in any of our lifetimes to create wealth. In some areas of the country, prices are what they were 20 years ago and some areas (as we already discussed, my area of metro Detroit) are at values you have not seen in 50 years! As we already discussed, there is still a huge demand for rental housing in most parts of the country and most of those rent levels have stayed at what they were at their highs.

It is now possible to buy properties at 1960 levels and rent them out for 2012 rent levels. It's almost like we have entered a real estate "Twilight Zone." If we were back in the 1960s and you could buy a property for $20,000 and rent it out for $800.00 a month would you do so assuming you had the money? The rents to value ratios are so far out of whack I keep wondering how long it will be before people start to realize the golden opportunity we have at our finger tips. I would submit to you that it is far safer to buy those properties today than it was back in the 60s. If we were really back in the 60s, time wise, you could not possibly hope to rent those homes for $800.00 per month as the average wage was far lower than it is now. Also, at that time, those properties had never been worth over $100,000 and most people could never even conceive that one day they would sell for over $100,000. Today, however, these homes have a history of selling for over $100,000, so the idea that they one day could again sell for those amounts is not altogether out of the question. After all, the population is used to those prices and they already make enough money to support those higher values.

The market is so oversold and overloaded with foreclosures that I would submit to you that the prices are due for a bounce within 2 to 3 years. The glut of foreclosures must be absorbed back into private hands of savvy real estate investors before prices can rebound. Nobody has a crystal ball to be able to predict these things, but we do have some powerful facts that would support this as a reasonable conclusion:

1. Banks have restricted money flow to the real estate market, which has further fueled the fall of prices. That will change as it has always done in the past. This is not the first time banks have gone through a time of pull back and will not be the last. They are always followed by a time of easy money that will fuel the pent up demand that exists currently across the country.

2. Many people are not qualified (in the traditional mortgage market anyway) to qualify for a mortgage, even though they have income and maybe even a small down payment, due to past credit issues. Most of those issues are foreclosures and also bankruptcies that have been occurring by the millions over the last several years. So, many people would love to own a home again but feel they are shut out of the market. When

people realize that once they are past those problems for two to three years, many will be able to get conventional financing again, and they will be buying in force. They will buy the same homes they lost for 50 to 75% of their former values. This will (assuming the glut of foreclosures is absorbed by then) fuel prices in the upward direction.

3. When the unemployment rate begins to fall consistently, that means consumers have more confidence about the economy and will begin to think of long-term purchases, such as homes. It is my personal opinion and probably one of the only political notes I will make in this book but it seems to me the way to begin to get that rate down is to STOP PAYING PEOPLE NOT TO WORK FOR YEARS AT A TIME!! The unemployment insurance program was never supposed to be a long-term solution to unemployment but a short-term stopgap measure to give income to people until they found another job. That system is one of the most abused government plans ever developed. I suspect that if people knew they got that income for 6 to 9 months maximum, their butts would be out looking for work or starting new ventures to provide income for their families. I have seen hundreds of people (that is just me personally) abuse that program by milking it for all they can before getting serious about obtaining a job. Even worse, they go back just long enough to qualify again and then somehow always seem to lose that job. Even in my area of metro Detroit, which has higher than average unemployment figures, I see tens of thousands of jobs advertised. I have gone through my own tough times where my income dried up for quite awhile but I did not get unemployment (my choice as to how I structure my financial affairs) and that forced me to get creative and

aggressive in a big hurry. I ended up getting something up and running that was far better than my other income stream that it had to replace. I would not have done that nearly as quickly if I had been collecting unemployment for 3 years. Alright I am off of my soapbox. The bottom line is get the country back to work with unemployment at 5% or less and watch what happens to housing values.

4. Here are a few things that I believe are signaling a turnaround in the next few years to metro Detroit real estate. Since we have spent some time discussing that market in particular, lets talk about some indications that metro Detroit may be gearing up for a rebound in real estate values. We have elected a new mayor for the city of Detroit, which was desperately needed. Even though we do not invest in the city, it is important to the suburbs that Detroit has a turnaround. That was simply not possible with the previous mayor (who is now in prison) and many of the former city council members (some of whom are in prison or have been accused of corruption on large levels) in charge of the government. The new mayor is Dave Bing, who is a former Detroit Piston and a very successful businessman in his post NBA days. I believe he is trying to make some difficult decisions to try and put Detroit back on a track of growth and prosperity. It will take many years for that to happen and will more than likely require several good administrations for that to come to pass. I do believe they are taking the first critical steps as of this writing. Detroit is known as the motor city for a reason and most of you know it is still the auto capital of the world. Since the difficult financial times of a few years ago and after bankruptcy and restructuring of a couple of the big three, U.S. automakers have made a dramatic turnaround back to profitability. They have paid back or are paying back

the government on a timely basis and are starting to show consistently profitable quarters. This is important not only financially for the area but also psychologically for the entire state of Michigan. When autoworkers feel better about the long-term prospects for their jobs, they buy goods and services and new homes. The Michigan economy is also finally starting to diversify and look at other industries for revenue besides the auto industry. They are starting to practice on a macroeconomic scale a wealth principle I have been teaching people for years to practice in their own lives. That concept is Multiple Wealth Streams. If you are totally dependent on only one source of income, you are subject to severe downturns when that source of income changes. Well Michigan is finally learning this concept (takes bureaucrats longer to figure these things out), and is working on bringing world-class medical facilities to the area as well as the movie industry, which is starting to produce and film many projects in Michigan. Another industry we have always had but never really marketed well is tourism. You will be hard-pressed to find a better getaway during the summer months than in Michigan. The Great Lakes are fantastic and provide picturesque views as well as dozens of activities that are unique to Michigan.

5. Another positive note in Michigan is a new governor in office, which was desperately needed. The jury is still out to see if his new polices will create jobs and bring this economy back in the few years to come. The last administration was a complete disaster and within eight years, dropped Michigan to the bottom of many economic lists. We needed fresh eyes and some new ideas, and I hope this administration will be the one to start to bring this state back to the leader it should be and has been in the past. They are making some difficult

decisions and are coming under fire because everyone wants change... until the change negatively affects them and forces them to change.

Now until these factors come to pass and have some time to play out we have an absolute gold mine for savvy real estate investors to be able to buy quality properties at rock bottom prices and hold them for great cash returns and cash flows. If you were able to acquire 20 properties over the next 4 to 7 years and values did not head up much, you would be generating $16,000 per month of gross rental income, which would translate to about $10,000 per month of net income in your pocket after all expenses. That is a great pension plan, by anyone's definition! When you combine this simple strategy with Perpetual Financing and flow your rental income back through your properly designed policy you will not only achieve great cash flow but you will also, over a very short period of time, defeat one of the biggest downsides of real estate ownership... LIQUIDITY!

If you fund your policy with enough money (either right away or over a period of several years) you will be able to buy your first few properties by borrowing the money out of your policy and paying the policy loan back as if you had borrowed that money from an outside lender. So let's take a look at our $100,000 of cash value in our life insurance contract and assume we borrow out the money to buy those 4 $25,000 properties and lease them out for $800 but get to keep $500 after expenses. That means in one year you have taken all of the money out of one property and made it liquid. Over a few short years you can have all your money out of the properties in the form of rental income but you will still own the properties free and clear and they will be producing money for you for years to come. They are not illiquid anymore because you solved that challenge of real estate investment by using the Perpetual Finance System.

This is your time to be able to acquire your own cash flow machines that will spit out money every month for you in the years to come. Never have you been able to buy such quality homes in nice areas for such low prices and rent them out for such fantastic cash-on-cash returns. Make some wise investments today and they will pay you income for life. This is money that comes in month after month whether or not you are there to work. You could disappear on a first-class vacation for the whole month and when you get back you will have income being paid to you. When it is done properly, you can turn the management of those properties over to professionals and let them handle all the details and 95% of the headaches that can occur when you own income-producing real estate. I made the mistake years ago of managing my own properties and not letting professionals handle the details. I did this mainly because my profit margins were so small on the rents that I could not afford to pay a management company to run the show. Well, in this new economy the cash flow and profit margins are far higher and there is no excuse not to get professional help. This will allow you to own dozens of income properties with very little to do from your end except keep tabs on the management company and make sure they are doing an effective job of leasing and maintaining your properties. This gives you the ability to produce true passive income. Passive income is so much better than earned income because you do the work once but you get paid for years to come.

This is one of the main reasons that now is the time to acquire cash producing assets like income properties and not focus so much on flipping the homes. I know flipping is sexy and when done properly can produce big chunks of money, but it is not passive income. You always have to be hustling for the next deal to turn. You have a high paying job but not passive income. If you disappear for the month, you are more than likely not buying or selling any properties and therefore your income is not consistent. You can flip in any market but this is the most unique time in history to acquire cash producing income properties at ridiculous prices and lease them out for great rent to value ratios. Set up a lifetime money machine and your pension plan today.

My team actually has a program set up where we do everything for you and you collect checks. We find the deals, analyze the deals, make offers on the deals, close the deals, rehab the deals, screen and place the tenant, manage the property long-term, and eventually sell the property for you when you are ready. You have to provide the cash but we provide everything else. We have clients who will own dozens of cash flowing properties that will enable them to retire from their jobs and spit off income every month for them to use as they see fit. What an incredible time to give yourself choices and options. If you can set this up and not spend the income for a while, you have the potential to retire with millions of dollars tax-free by combining cash flow real estate with Perpetual Financing.

I hope you will truly seize this opportunity that is at your feet. The people that do will set up a cash flow machine that will pump money into their lives for years to come. The people that read this and don't act upon the information will be kicking themselves in 10 years when they are still working for their money instead of their money working for them, and providing security and choices for their futures. Get in touch with me and my team through our real estate site at www.recashflowmachine.com and set up a no obligation trip to our town to look at killer deals. See you in metro Detroit soon.

Chapter Eleven

"TRIPLE DIP" YOUR WAY TO GENERATIONAL WEALTH

Marketing Tip: If you would like to generate a lot of leads in your real estate investment business there is not a need to use anything else except for this "ugly yellow letter." I was shown this and it has generated tons of leads for me and many successful real estate investment transactions. Mail it to the proper lists such as pre foreclosures, probates, expired listings, and divorces, among others and you will get a ton of calls. Get an example of this lead generating magnet for free. Simply visit <u>www.perpetualfinancingsystem.com/ yellow</u> for your free download.

This chapter is the reason for this book and training system. I found two huge wealth creators that work fantastic by themselves. When you combine them together, both strategies get turbo-charged and make each strategy stronger. The first strategy is Perpetual Financing, which is a way to redirect the money flow in your life. Instead of all the payments leaving your family forever, you create your own financing pool through a properly designed insurance policy. Then you make a commitment to utilize that financing pool (insurance policy) and pay back the loan to the insurance company with interest. When you utilize this strategy at the basic level, it is, in my opinion, one of the biggest wealth creators the world has ever seen. In using your own money instead of your local lender, you pick up all the principle and interest you would have paid back the bank. You also still have control and ownership of the asset. Let's use a simple car example.

The old way of doing business would have you doing the following:

- $25,000 car bought using a 5 year car loan from Bank of America
- 5 years into this program you now own the car free and clear
- The car is worth around $5,000 and that is what you have left after making $29,000 worth of payments ($25,000 principle and about $4,000 worth of interest) back to the bank. $5,000 residual value of the car

Now look at the numbers below and where you would be if you would have funded your own policy with $25,000 worth of cash value to start your financing pool.

- $25,000 car bought using a 5 year loan from the insurance company with your money inside the insurance policy collateralizing the debt
- 5 years of making payments back into this program you now own the car free and clear
- The car is worth the same $5,000 as in the example above

- Now because you used the power of the insurance policy, your policy has the $25,000 cash back into the policy but also the $4,000 worth of interest. So now you have $29,000 in cash back into your policy plus your $5,000 residual value of your car. Your loan from the insurance company is now satisfied and your cash value is freed up to be used again if you wish to collateralize another loan

Which is better out of these two examples?

With example number one, you have $5,000 worth of assets and have lost $29,000 worth of payments that you will never see again.

With example number two, you have $29,000 in cash plus your $5,000 car for a total asset value of $34,000. You also have growth in the account that was added from the insurance company when they paid out the guaranteed growth and if they paid out dividends.

Now some alleged guru will tell you yes, but what would have happened if you would have taken your $25,000 and put it in the market in that amount of time? The answer is I don't know, neither do you, and neither do they. Please don't fall for that same old tired argument of "average rates of return" as you know better than that now. The fact is that the stock market only grew at a little over 5% from 1900 to 2000 and there were many blocks of time during that time where it was way down. Also most of that growth would be taxed it outside of a qualified plan unlike growth inside the insurance policy.

You will never get me to believe that you should have taken the $25,000 and put in the market instead of using it as a financing vehicle. I can guarantee my results by using that money if I just pay it back. The stock market is a crapshoot and has many other downsides. Why can't banks put their money into the market? The answer is because it is deemed too risky. So if it is too risky for them, why do tens of millions of Americans have the bulk of their money in the market? As we already discussed in a previous chapter, it is because of the giant Wall Street conspiracy. You don't need to be a part of it and can totally control your financial future with certainty instead of uncertainty.

That example of the car above is very powerful but it relies on you utilizing your own financing pool with your own money and paying the payments back out of your own funds. What if it were possible to get someone else to make your car payments? If that were possible you become a financing pool and the results are even far greater than in the car example. Also if what you buy appreciates instead of depreciates like a car you end up with much more wealth. What if that $25,000 car after five years was worth $40,000 instead of $5,000? Now we are talking about serious wealth creation and a rapid rate. Unfortunately cars do not work that way but cash flow real estate can and has many times in the past appreciated dramatically. Investment of any kind has risk but the risk with cash flow property when done as we have described should be minimal.

Now instead of using the car example, let's use the $25,000 house example. As we already discussed, it is now possible to get cash producing properties for less than cars! We buy that $20,000 home and put $5,000 of repairs into the property. We borrow the money from our financing pool (you know by now we are talking about borrowing money from the insurance company and using our funds to collateralize that loan) to acquire and repair the home. Now instead of a $400 car payment that we make from our own funds into the policy, we now pay back $500 into the policy but that $500 actually comes from our tenants who are more than happy to make us rich. So now our tenants are growing our wealth tax-free by putting that money back into the policy and when done properly, those payments also qualify for guaranteed growth and dividends. Those funds can also be used to pay down the lien against your cash value of your policy. So if you don't need the income from your buildings to live on yet, use the rent to pay back the insurance company and grow wealth exponentially. Here is the "Triple Dip":

1. Your loan from the insurance company buys a quality piece of real estate that produces large cash-on-cash returns.

2. You see, the way we set up polices, when you borrow out the money you still get guaranteed growth and dividends (when dividends are paid out by the insurance company) on that same money. Now you borrow out your funds to buy cash producing assets that flow more money back into our policies. That money qualifies for additional growth tax-free inside of our policies or can be used to pay down the loan to the insurance company freeing up our cash value to take additional loans if we choose.

3. Here is another dip of your money. When you set up your policy and then borrow out the money from the insurance company you will pay the money back with interest. If you had borrowed the money from a regular bank, hard money lender, or a private lender, would the interest you pay on that loan be tax deductible as a cost of owning that property? I am not a tax expert or a CPA but my tax attorney tells me that the interest would be deductible as a normal course of business. (Make sure you consult with your own tax professionals.) So if we are borrowing money from the insurance company's general fund and have to pay interest on it, do we get to claim the interest as an expense? The answer (again according to my tax attorney) is yes we can! If that money was borrowed out for a legitimate business purpose such as real estate investment, for example, then the interest you pay is deductible. Please check

with your own tax experts. It might also be advisable to set up an entity that is set up for financing only. So it would look like this: Policy owner borrows the money from the insurance company at a low rate and then you loan the money to another entity that you control at a little higher rate, which is probably a finance company. The financing entity pays the owner of the policy back, who in turn pays back the insurance company, so you maintain an arm's length transaction for tax purposes. Yes, you write the interest off and because of the way we set up the policy that interest is going toward your cash value and building your wealth. Since you control the pool of funds, why not charge yourself a little higher rate than normal? This puts a whole different light on paying back loans. I don't mind paying so much if those payments go toward helping grow my wealth and not the bank's.

Now you see why this strategy is the "Triple Dip" of funds. Your same money is working three times as hard as it would otherwise. This is an important point to understand. Take the time and read it again and make sure you understand this simple yet powerful strategy. Then get some quality tax advice from your own tax experts and implement this in your life immediately, if not sooner. We can help you every step of the way.

Part of this chapter title says create *generational wealth* for a good reason. When you understand the Perpetual Financing concept and implement it in your own life, you are starting a wealth program that will last for generations to come. (this assumes you make timely premium payments and are a good steward of the financing pool you have created) This is not just about leaving behind tax-free wealth in the form of death benefits. It is also not just about leaving behind dozens of free and clear pieces of real estate that produce income for years. It is really much more than either of those two events. You have the opportunity to show your children and grandchildren how money really works and how they can have a great life with many options if they will adopt this philosophy and put it to work inside of their families. If you don't embed it in their DNA then all they will do is inherit a bunch of money, live like rock stars for a couple years, and then be broke. Wealth is too powerful to just squander and many squandering is easy to do, especially when it has not been earned.

This is your chance to teach your future generations how to start foundations, charities, and other philanthropic endeavors. When you are not tied down to have to make just a living, then a whole other world opens up to you as do possibilities. Teach them to be productive and grow the family wealth safely and predictably. During this time, they can also adopt great causes of yours or their own. They can be a huge asset to their fellow man and leave behind a family mark that will help many thousands of people (and hopefully millions of people) to have better lives and opportunities.

Most families are so concerned with just paying the bills that they lose sight of actually making a serious difference in many people's lives for hundreds of years to come. If you will adopt his system today, teach it to your future generations, and help them implement the program, the sky is the limit. Start to think bigger about money and see what you can achieve.

Chapter Twelve

GETTING STARTED WITH YOUR CASH FLOW MACHINES TODAY

I would like to use our final pages together to try and tie this all together and give you a step-by-step action plan to get your Perpetual Financing System and your real estate cash flow machine up and running. This is the time when I ask you to stop being a reader and start being a doer. I mentioned that I have had the good fortune to train thousands of people in live events all over North America. There is almost no major city in the United States or Canada that I have not been to for a weekend training event. I love to train and teach people and I am a voracious seeker of knowledge.

We have all been taught that knowledge is power. Just get more knowledge and you will make more money and be a happier person. That is a load of garbage. As we discussed before, it is not just about knowledge. It is about specialized knowledge combined with a powerful action plan. Without the action plan, you will just spin your wheels and learn a lot of "stuff." There is nothing worse than a broke know-it-all! I have encountered many in my travels. They are not only broke financially but broke spiritually and that is why they are constantly learning more useless facts and figures. Somehow they reason that if they know more they are superior and happy to be just that, even if it is just in their own minds.

They never actually take any real action on the things they learn. They never really throw their hat in the ring to actually achieve anything. I am begging you not to let that happen to you. The strategies in this book are just too good not to act on right away. If you don't take a positive first step right away then you are in real danger of just letting this go away and never getting started. I will give you a step-by-step plan to get this up and running as we wrap up shortly. Don't be just a thinker, doing is much more important. Be a man or woman of action and do what is needed to set you and generations to come up for fantastic, productive, and profitable lives. This is your right and destiny.

Think of how fortunate you are to have been born in the United States or to have immigrated here to this huge land of opportunity. You are meant for greatness. You are meant to matter to other people. You are meant to be productive and achieve. You are meant to enjoy the fruits of your labor and have a great home, cars, vacations, money in the bank, family, friends, etc. You can also start foundations and charities that will outlive your physical body. You can donate money and time to worthy causes of your choice. Let someone else be small and happy with the scraps from the table. Let others cry and moan about how bad life is and why they can't get ahead. You came for the full banquet and you can have it, if you will do what most are not willing to do to be successful.

So let's get started by first deciding how much money we would like to fund your financing pool with out of the gate. That is a personal decision but you might want to look at what banks do with their money. As we discussed earlier, many of the world's largest banks keep 20 to 40% of their tier one core assets inside of life insurance policies. Maybe that is a good place for you to start. If you have $300,000 worth of investible assets maybe you might consider putting $100,000 to $150,000 into your properly designed policy to start. Many people ask me if they can "roll over" their qualified plans to an insurance policy. The answer is no, you cannot do that without tax and penalty implications. For more details on this, to find out what the penalty might be, and how to use qualified plans to fund your financing insurance policy, call our team today. Even though we may not be able to roll over those qualified plans without penalty, there are other options for you to guarantee your principle and receive predictable, safe, strong growth. My team is set up to give you proper direction in this matter.

Many people do not have those kinds of resources so they think cannot participate. Nothing could be further from the truth. You can start with a very small amount of money and build your financing pool over a several year period. Start from where you can and go from there. You can also put money in monthly to your policy and build it like you would a qualified plan. Be patient and do what you can to get started, but do start.

Now once you have an idea of the kind of money you have to get this started, then get in contact with my office to have a free no obligation illustration run for you and have a 30-minute consultation with a Perpetual Financing Expert. Let me also say that if this book was given to you by someone who is teaching you this concept and is hoping you will start a policy with them, then by all means go back to that person for help. If they know how to set these polices up and specialize in them, then please let them help you get it set up. We have enough business of our own that we don't need to steal potential clients from someone who is supporting this book and training program. If that does not apply to you, then by all means, contact our office to schedule your 30-minute consultation and start to run some real numbers. We work with people from all over the United States and Canada to get their financing polices set up and operating. Not only do we help you set them up, but you will also learn how to maximize their use and how to make them grow faster.

Once our 30-minute call is complete, we will have obtained from you some basic information so that we may run a policy illustration, which is, in effect, our set of numbers on your own policy to see how it performs over the years. We will have set up with you a follow-up webinar to go over those numbers and get any questions you may still have answered at that point. The next step is to take your application and get the ball rolling on getting your policy set up. We generally will have one of our client care providers call you back and take your application over the phone and then fax or email it to you for your signature.

The next step is to process that application and work with you and the insurance carriers to get them the information they need to approve your application as quickly as possible. This process will require a set of medical screenings to qualify you for the insurance. A nurse will come to your home and take a medical application and get basic medical tests done on the spot. The application, along with your medicals, goes to the proper insurance carrier based on the type and size of policy you are looking to set up. The underwriting process varies from carrier to carrier but is usually about 2 to 3 weeks or so to come out of underwriting. Most come out approved, some come back approved but rated (higher risk due to medical condition so the insurance portion of the policy is a little higher), approved at a preferred rate (meaning you are in better than average shape so your cost of insurance is a little lower), or rejected due to a few different reasons.

If you have a current whole life policy or variable policy that has cash value, you may want to consider exchanging that policy and its cash value into your new policy because it will be structured very differently than those polices. WARNING, WARNING, WARNING!! If you have a Universal policy or Variable policy and you think it is set up for perpetual financing… you are very wrong. Those policies are built to fail and will almost always self implode on themselves after a number of years.

The reason is that those polices are built with an underlying term policy (usually a 20 year term) which is inexpensive at the beginning of the policy but get very expensive later. I had a 70 year old man come into my class one time whose universal policy premium just went to almost $65,000 a year to keep the policy in force. You see, he bought the policy when he was 49 and for 20 years the policy's underlying insurance was pretty inexpensive. After the 20-year time frame, the man now had to pay insurance based on his attained age and now paid annual renewable term rates based on being 70 years old. He closed down the policy because that underlying cost of insurance is a kind of financial cancer that eats the policy from within. Most of those policies come with a no growth guarantee and if you borrow money from them and the market takes a dive your money could be at risk. This became a problem early on in the creation of these policies and people started to realize that these style policies were really a glorified mutual fund inside of an insurance vehicle. So now you can obtain policies where your principle balance is guaranteed and they have supposed growth guarantees but just understand for now that those policies are not much better than the first generation of polices they are trying to replace. In these types of products the risk is put on you for those policies to perform and they are market driven. So many times you will see these kinds of polices illustrated based on the "market averaging" 7% compound interest. However, as we all know now the market does not grow at a compound rate and to truly average something you have to take into account the down years as well as the up years. However, those illustrations show monies increasing as if they were compounding and never take into account the dips and downturns. So the illustrations are hocus pocus and the polices are very complicated. As my mom used to say you have to be a "Philadelphia" lawyer to understand them and that should be another warning flag to you how risky these kinds of policies are for your financial future. Most of our illustrations are 9 to 11 pages and are actually quite simple to understand with a little knowledge of terms. I have seen illustrations from variable polices that are 35 pages long! That is way too complex and risky for my tastes. In a Perpetual Financing style of policy the risk is transferred away from you and the markets to the insurance company. They have the risk of the principle guarantee and the growth and it is not dependant on any outside market forces. One of the big reasons you are considering setting one of these programs up is for security so why would you risk that with a variable product? We don't believe you should and we will not put you into that kind of casino product.

Again, as we said before, if you are in one of those (many of our clients used to be as well, so no worries) we can simply exchange you out of one and into a new and properly designed policy. When we do a "roll over" it is called a 1035 (named after the IRS code where you can find the details) exchange of one insurance policy for another. This will make sure there are no income tax implications by closing the old policy down and exchanging the money from that old policy to your new policy. PLEASE DON'T CANCEL ANY POLICES UNTIL YOUR NEW POLICY IS 100% APPROVED. IF YOU VIOLATE THIS WARNING YOU MAY FIND YOURSELF WITH NO INSURANCE PROTECTION FOR YOUR FAMILY AND THAT IS COUNTER-PRODUCTIVE TO WHAT WE ARE TRYING TO ACCOMPLISH.

Assuming your application is approved, you will then work with our client care specialists to get your policy delivered and closed with appropriate papers signed. You are now the proud owner of a properly designed insurance policy that can be used as a financing pool if you wish. Now you are ready to start using those funds and take policy loans with your cash value from your policy as the collateral. You can request a loan with a phone call and usually a one-page sheet of paper to access the funds. The check will be sent out in a couple days and some carriers will even wire you the funds directly to your bank account.

Now, if you have some debt with normal banks or finance companies, it is time to refinance with your own pool of funds. Simply pay off that debt with your loan from your policy and begin to start making the same payments (or more if you wish) to the insurance company which will free up your cash value to be used again in the future if you wish. Before your eyes, you have just shifted the money flow out of your life back into your life and started to create wealth for you instead of for the banks. You are now in control of your finances and your financial future. You are now out of the grip of the banks and finance companies. Now if you pay a late fee, it will be to yourself and not to the banks. I am so excited for you because this is within your grasp if you will just take action to make it a reality.

Now that you have the policy set up, you just need to make premium payments (at whatever level you choose) to keep your policy open and growing. Make sure you treat funds taken out of that account as a true loan and pay them back with interest. Don't steal from your financing pool and your financial future. There will come a time when you do not have to make premium payments out of your own fresh money. In other words, there will be enough growth from guarantees and dividends that the premium can be taken out of the policy and it will still grow! You will also be able to take out policy loans income tax-free and not have to worry about making payments. That will be here before you know it, but during your serious money making years, make payments back to your policy and build more tax-free wealth. So get the policy set up, get as much money in as you can as fast as you can, pay back any loans with interest, and you're guaranteeing your financial security.

I would like to now talk about setting up multiple policies for you and your family. Let's assume for now that you are 100% on board with this program and are going to make it a major part of your wealth creation and protection efforts. We will assume you set up your first policy but now wish you would have put in more money, or it is several years later and you are putting a lot of money into your policy. This is when you have to make sure you don't M.E.C. out the policy. M.E.C. stands for "modified endowment contract" and is something we do not want for our life insurance policies.

In short, an M.E.C. is a status that a life insurance contract can change to instead of just a life insurance contract. Many years ago, before the implementation of M.E.C. limits by the Internal Revenue Service it was possible to put a ton of money into a life insurance contract without having to have a high death benefit. In other words, you could shelter a bunch of money from income taxes for life inside of a policy but you could have a very low life insurance death benefit. People were not doing this for the insurance aspect of these contracts but as a pure tax dodge. To this day, according to insurance executives I have spoken with, there are old contracts out there through which people has $500,000 in cash value but only a $300,000 death benefit. Those contracts were grandfathered in before the M.E.C. limits were put in place. Wealthy people used life insurance policies as a total tax dodge and not really at all for the insurance.

Since the institution of M.E.C. limits, you can still put in large amounts of cash inside a policy, but now you must have a correspondingly high amount of life insurance. So just for an example, if you would like to dump in $100,000 of cash into your banking policy you might need a $1,500,000 death benefit, to conform to the M.E.C limits. We will build your policy so it does not M.E.C. out according to the insurance company's own software program that has all the ratios already put into the program. Now let's assume you dumped in $100,000 this year and want to flow through $20,000 in annual premium to build cash value quickly. We will build your illustration to allow you to do that, but we must make sure you will qualify for that amount of insurance. There are ratios that we must conform to based on income and/or net worth as to how much life insurance you can qualify for inside of your policy. I won't bore you with all the details, since who really cares? It is my team's job to know what those ratios are and build your policy accordingly.

If your policy becomes an M.E.C., you lose the tax benefits of the policy and will be subject to 10% penalties for withdrawals as well. So we will build it not to M.E.C. and the insurance carrier will work with you during the life of the policy to advise you on M.E.C limits and how to stay under them. If you want to put more money into your policy and that amount will trigger an M.E.C. then we obviously don't put that extra money in until next year.

That brings us back to multiple polices scenario. If you want to put more money into your policy, without turning into an M.E.C., then consider starting a new policy either on you or a spouse. You can even open up policies on a child where the death benefit is on them (of course you pray it is never used in your lifetime) but you control the cash value as the owner of the policy. So you could have several polices on yourself, your spouse, and on each child. This is a way to get more money into polices than any one person could normally qualify for, and providing insurance on all your family that will stick with them the rest of their lives. You can own a policy on anyone you have an insurable interest in such as family members, employees, and partners. If you have any doubt if an insurable interest exists between you and another party, get in touch with my team to discuss your situation.

Now let's assume we put $5,000 a year into a policy on each of our two minor children but we own all the cash value. We have just set those children up with their own financing pools and insurance for their lifetimes. They will be tax-free millionaires as long as those premiums are paid and they are good stewards of that pool of funds. You could pay those premiums for a number of years and then borrow out the money to help you with your retirement. Then, as the child takes over the premiums, that cash value is theirs and will grow with them throughout their lives. These types of policies will become tax free compounding machines over those years as long as you train the children when they are older how to use these tremendous vehicles.

Now the last part of this chapter is if you decide to use your funds to invest in high cash flow properties as we discussed in a previous chapter. Now you are going to take your newly formed financing pool and start to use the power of volume and velocity, as we discussed earlier. You can now borrow out those funds from the policy (remember you can't borrow out all of the money you put in because there are some costs of setting this program up, such as the cost insurance and commissions to the agents). My average client gets about 70 to 90% initial cash value from day one depending on how much they fund the policy with to start. You give up access to a small portion of the money in the initial few years but very soon you will have more money in the account than you have put into the policy and if you wish could acquire high quality properties in solid areas that cash flow for you.

Go back and study the 876 plan we talked about in detail in chapter 9. Understand that whole program and realize you are just a few short years from having a real estate cash flow machine that will pump out money every month whether you are there or not. This is true passive income for your family. This is so much better than a pension. When you put money into a pension plan and then start taking withdrawals, you only get income for your lifetime and your spouse's lifetime. When you and your spouse both die, the income stops forever and the company keeps the original wealth block that created that income stream. With this kind of income, you get it for your life, and when you die, you leave the income and the assets behind for your family or charities.

The income from your financing pool is also far superior to a traditional pension plan. You get to take income out of your policy income tax-free and when you die, you leave behind a bigger death benefit that your family can use to create lifelong income streams and security. This is the way to long-term, sustainable wealth. These systems and strategies have the power to change your family's well being for generations to come. The control resides with you and not the stock market. By all means, invest in the stock market if you have a desire to do so. Invest in businesses if you wish, but make sure you are true to your pool of funds you have set up to loan out and use this unique time in history to acquire real estate cash flow machines that provide true passive income and a chance at large backend equities when the market prices turn around again.

Surround yourself with like-minded people and network with movers and shakers constantly. Your network will support you and help you build wealth and opportunity. The old adage *you become who you hang out with* has much validity. If you are around people who are critical and skeptical, you run the risk of letting them suck the life out of your dreams. People love to steal your dreams and rain on your parade. You might as well get used to the fact that you think differently than 97% of the people who will be around you every day. You will make the average person (especially friends and family members) uncomfortable. They will see you going for your dreams and goals and it will bother them that you are trying to attain success. Most of them have long since given up on success because it was not laid down at their front door. When they actually had to get out of their comfort zone, they cashed in their chips and took the path of least resistance instead. Most paths of least resistance lead to mediocrity and not achievement. Pay the naysayers no mind as they will always try to drag you down. This is why it is critical to read good books and listen to great information from achievers every day. Watching reality TV will get you nowhere and just listening to music is not the answer (although if you talk to people who know me well, they will tell you I am a human jukebox and listen to the radio often) to being a success in life. I always have a motivational and training program with me at all times. Now I have them on my smart phone and can access them any time I have some down time or am en route somewhere. I love it and when I don't listen to them regularly I can literally see my productivity go down. Start every day with some positive information from achievers of your choice and watch your income rise along with your happiness level.

Make it a priority to attend quality real estate and business trainings. Use them not only for top-notch education from people who are achieving great things, but also as a time to recharge your battery. I love attending seminars as a student because they have changed my life. Not only has my income gone from zero to the top 1 percent of income earners in the country, they have changed my attitude and thought process. You get to hang around people who are doers or soon-to-be doers and their attitude is generally far better than your average friend or family member. I recommend you go out of town for a seminar at least twice a year. When you are not in class during the day, use the evening to dream and set goals for the upcoming quarter and for the rest of your life. Also use the evening to network with like minded people and build relationships that could be profitable for all involved. Devise a business plan, set up a power team, and make a very strong step-by-step 7-day plan for when you return home.

If you see a program you can invest in that makes sense for your business, go ahead and invest in it. Yes, I sell programs and it is a revenue stream for my business, but I also have been a purchaser of programs many dozens of times. If you can get just one or two good ideas that you can actually use in your business, it will be money well spent. You pay for the information once but you get to use it for the rest of your life. Maybe one day you will feel confident enough and have enough specialized knowledge to develop your own training program. If you have success in a specific area, consider putting together a program to show people how they can achieve better results as well.

My team and I put on a Perpetual Financing and Private Money Boot Camp several times and year and it is one of the best ways you can spend 4 days, mastering this topic and learning so much more. Check out our website at www.perpetualfinancingsystem.com for the next date and invest in that program. Our students rave about it and come back with friends and family members. You will also find a home study package and other training systems available on that site.

Think of ever more creative ways you can use your private financing pool to create wealth. One of the best ways to create great returns safely is to really use your financing pool as a high interest rate source to be loaned out to other investors. There is a multibillion-dollar industry called private or hard money lending. This is a world where traditional banks, credit unions, and finance companies do not operate and it is a booming opportunity. This has been the best time in my 20 plus years in business to start loaning out money at what we call hard money rates. Many times I have loaned out money at 5 points (a point is 1 percentage point of the loan amount) and 15% payable in monthly interest-only payments for 12 months, and then the loan balloons and the principle becomes due and payable.

There are many more things you need to know about how to be a private lender or maybe you want to be on the opposite side of the fence and access the boat-loads of private money that is available to fund real estate and business deals. Please don't think if you need funds that the banks are the only, or even the best, choice. There are many people who would love to make a sound, secure loan to you to acquire a great piece of real estate or a good business with a lot of potential. I have put together an entire training program on CD that explains this private lending business in great depth. You will be able to loan out your money at high interest rates and/or access the private wealth pool I have been discussing. It is combined with much more in depth training on using Perpetual Financing to build and protect wealth. I highly recommend you make the investment in this cutting edge training program. To have it shipped to your door simply go to www.perpetualfinancingsystem.com and click on the order button, and we will ship it out to you right away.

Using your policy as a financing source for private or "hard money" is very safe and very profitable when done properly. We loan very low loan to values on the property or the business to create safety. We also loan that money and maintain more control than the average bank does. This system will turbo-charge your private financing pool and you can use someone else's money to build your wealth. This is the essence of financing and why it has been around for over 5,000 years. Make a commitment that you are going to do whatever is needed to increase your knowledge about using your own pool of funds to create generational wealth.

Financing is a business and when you treat your pool of funds as a business, it will pay you like a business, and tax-free to boot. I hope you will build wealth using many vehicles over your lifetime and always maintain multiple wealth streams in your life at all times.

If you have great success in real estate, stocks, business, or anything else, that is fantastic. The same time you're building wealth with those endeavors your financing pool will be creating tax-free wealth by funding those endeavors, like any other lenders would, and getting paid back for their loans. That financing pool will also be able to fund things for other people that make smart business loans for your company. Since you will be loaning out your money as a principle, you should not need a license to loan out money. It is only when you are loaning other people's money out and collecting fees for doing so, that you will need a license through your state. That being said, I recommend that you double check with a really good attorney who handles loans and the like in your area. You will need a good attorney and closing agent anyway, so why not find one in advance and make sure you are doing everything to adhere to your states laws?

You are sitting on a gold mine if you will continue your training and start to implement these strategies in your own life. This better not be a book that you read and then never take any action with the information. If that turns out to be the case for you, your time has been wasted by reading it and not acting. If you consider doing that, go back to the beginning of the book and look at the number you have paid out in payments, and then look again at that number doubled. Then compare it to how much money you have saved for your later years, and if they are not even close, how long are you going to wait and have those numbers never catch one another? Take control of your financial future right now and begin your journey to true wealth and financial independence.

If you would like my help in your journey and would like my team of experts to work on getting your policy designed and built properly for you, call my office directly at **586 944 0794** or visit us on line and www.perpetualfinancingsystem.com and contact us from the site. You can even fill out a policy illustration request form on the next page and tear it off and use the instructions on the form to get it to us right away. Once we receive this filled out questionnaire, one of my associates will be in touch to see if we can be of help to you and your family.

Also if you missed it, go back to the beginning of the book and request your 3 free DVDs that will show you how to make, create, grow, and protect money for generations to come. We will rush you out that package right away.

Also if you are one of those high paying business owners we talked about before that would like to know how to dramatically reduce your bottom line federal tax obligation then go to www.perpetualfinancingsystem.com/taxreduction for a package to be shipped out to you right away. This is a game changer for you!

PERPETUAL FINANCING QUESTIONNAIRE

How did you find out about us?

_____

Name _____

Address_____

City_____State_____ Zip_____

Date of _____

Phone Number_____

Cell Number _____

E-mail _____

Annual Income _____

Profession, Business, or Job _____

How much would you like to put in the policy, year one, to fund your financing pool?

_____

How much annually would you like to flow through (contribute) the policy?

_____

What are your plans for your bank once it is funded?

_____

_____

_____

Do you have any current coverage for life insurance and, if yes, how much is the face amount?

_____

Is it term, whole life, universal life or a mixture?

_____

Would you like to do this as soon as possible or at a certain time in the future?

_____

Have you used tobacco in the last 12 months?

_____

Male or Female_____

    When completed email to colleen@perpetualfinancingsystem.com or fax to (586) 273-1507.

    We have talked a lot about using your new policy to buy income properties at record low prices and then renting them out for great, heavy cash flows and solid double digit returns on your money, year in and year out. You may choose to use that 7 to 8 year retirement plan to have a step-by-step plan on being able to get out of a job that is less than rewarding or even one you hate. To be able to do that you will need someone who has been eating, sleeping, and breathing real estate investment for over 20 years. You will need boots on the ground that you can trust to run your investments for you without you having to be there. My partners and I have that system already up and running for dozens of investors and you can tap into our system if you choose. We have the turnkey system just waiting for you to tap into, from finding, funding, closing, rehabbing, leasing out, to managing your investments, long-term. To find out more details and look at videos of existing clients and real-life deals, visit us on line at www.recashflowmachine.com. Take some time at that site and contact us from there to get your own real estate cash flow machine up and running.

    I want to thank you for taking the time to read this book and I hope you will put it into practice. I hope I have shown you some innovative ideas that you had not thought of or maybe knew about but had never acted upon. I have a passion for helping people achieve more than they thought possible. After you get involved with my company and have had some success, please send me a personal email telling me about your success and what this book or training program has meant to you and your family. It has been my pleasure writing this book and I hope to meet you someday over the phone or in person at a live event. Contact us today to get your future started right away. May your dreams become your reality!

Please read the following quote, as it is one of my favorites and I believe it to be spot on. Then prove your persistence by getting in contact with my office to get your Perpetual Wealth System up and running immediately.

"Nothing in the world can take the place of persistence. Talent will not; nothing is more common than unsuccessful men with talent. Genius will not; unrewarded genius is almost a proverb. Education will not; the world is full of educated derelicts. Persistence and determination alone are omnipotent. The slogan 'Press On!' has solved and always will solve the problems of the human race."

—Calvin Coolidge

ACKNOWLEDGEMENTS

When you undertake the writing of a book you don't really understand all that goes into the project until you are knee deep. That is probably why more people don't actually ever get a book published. I want to thank many people for the contribution either to this book or myself over the years. Along with my parents at the front of the book I wanted to thank my two sisters Jody and Mary for being supportive sisters and friends along with their husbands and my friends Joe and Mark.

I have too numerous of early mentors to include here but there were many who helped me realize there was much more available in life than what we are taught in the traditional world.

To my early clients I want to say thank you for helping me launch my first business. Thanks as well to my first partner Rick Sabol and his wife, my cousin Kim. We helped each other launch into a new world and we learned together as we went along changing both our lives for the better. Many people who worked with me on projects over the years: Joe Loduca, Sal Loduca, Brian Susko, Augie Tiseo, and countless JV partners and associates. Thanks you to Edna Bautista from Dynetech who gave me my first chance at public speaking and training which has lead to many great relationships and opportunities. Thanks to Stephen Libman for being a good friend and business associate. Thanks to Melvin Jackson, Tracie Taylor, Rick Henderson, and Tim Chaffin for helping me launch this program inside a major seminar company. Special thanks as well to Chris Lombardo and Tom McElroy for working with me to get this message out to their students and for changing people's lives.

Last and certainly not least are my current business associates Joe Militello who is my partner and friend at The Real Estate Cash Flow Machine. Greg Lozon for introducing me to new concepts and making me listen even when I thought I knew it all. Todd Avery for writing a great foreword and helping me bring this program to a new level to help more people. To all the people in our office who help us do what we do: Dave Jacobson, Colleen Zalewski, Marybeth Jamieson, Sandy Militello, Mike Estes, Bob Lynch and countless support staff.

In closing I want to thank God for allowing me to be born into a fantastic family in the greatest country in the world. Where else can a high school failure and college dropout climb the ladder of success? Thanks you also for allowing me to be born during the greatest time in history for opportunity. My wish is that everyone who reads this understands the unlimited potential they have and take action to seize the day and the rest of their life.

JOHN JAMIESON

Is a wealth strategist and serial entrepreneur who began in business at the age of twenty one. From there he went on to purchase many millions of dollars worth of investment real estate. John was also a success in the world of real estate brokerage having sold tens of millions of dollars worth of properties. He was a corporate sales trainer for Century 21 Real Estate Corporation helping other agents achieve their personal and sales goals.

John is a former REO agent who sold hundreds of properties for lending institutions and worked with many real estate investors to help them build their real estate portfolios. He is a sought after coach and mentor to investors and business people from all over the country.

After achieving success in his own business and investments John caught the attention of many national trainers. He was invited to help them teach wealth classes all over North America. John spoke for people like Donald Trump, Robert Allen, and the National Foreclosure Institute.

John launched Perpetual Wealth Systems and works with clients and students from all over North America showing them how to create guaranteed, tax free, generational wealth. John has continued to teach these concepts with the help of major seminar companies from all over the country. John has been an invited guest at many Rich Dad Poor Dad events since launching Perpetual Wealth Systems.

John considers himself a wealth educator and wealth strategist and delights in teaching people new concepts and then helping them implement them in their lives. He works with a team of top people from all over the country to provide a truly unique list of services from private banking, private pensions, private lending, and cash flow real estate.

He is a lifelong resident of Metro Detroit where he resides with his wife and sons. You can always connect with John at www.theperpetualwealthsystem.com and his members only site at www.perpetualwealthclub.com